"We build worlds in which we live our lives. Our personality is the part of our world that faces other people's worlds.

To create relationships, we must build bridges between our worlds. To do this successfully, we must understand the personality. "

Naomi Eklund – Author

Building Bridges Between Personality,

Introducing the Enneagram

Copyrights

Series:

Building Bridges Between Personality©

Personality as a purposeful interface to achieve purpose, prosperity, and improve relationships.

Book 1:

Introducing the Enneagram ©

(based on the work in Accessing the Enneagram, copyright 2017).

Copyright 2019

Naomi Eklund, Infinite Yes Productions, Inc.

ISBN: 978-0-578-46854-9

LCCN:

Infinite Yes Productions ™
Infinite Yes Coaching, Inc. ™
www.infiniteyesinc.com
www.infiniteyesproductions.com
naomi@infiniteyesinc.com

© Jachob Wolff Imagery

Building Bridges Through Personality cover.

All Images within the book and personality graphic pages.

Building Bridges Through Personality

Introducing the Enneagram

by

Naomi Eklund

Table of Contents

Contents

Introduction

Thank you for purchasing this book.

It is the first in a series of books designed to bring your ideas and information to make your life easier.

In my years of practice, the largest source of problems I have seen for people is lack of information, which inhibits your ability to make good choices. It is my hope to help you make good choices instead of having to clean up emotional, costly relationship messes.

We all have challenges in some area of our life that involves relationships. I have been coaching for 25 years and worked with people across the spectrum from stay-at-home parents to CEOs and EVPs of international companies. This gives me an insight that few have. The fact is, that most of our problems are rooted in relationship issues.

My niche is people and relationships, these are the foundation of our lives. From the time of our conception we are in a relationship. With our self, our environment, our parents and family. As life progresses, we define our lives based on relationships. Every part of our life is about how we relate, the way we relate is determined by our personality. This is most importantly, how we relate to ourselves.

Your life improves when you decide to open your eyes to the complex world of personality including its effect on relationships. Knowledge is power because, with it, you can make better choices.

It is my intention with my work, that we get ahead of the problem and preemptively choose to thrive.

Author's confession: *I am amazed at our human capacity to learn and grow and overwhelmed by how much we seem to need or choose to learn from suffering. In running a business for 25 years, I had to do little advertising because of the volume of referrals. Everyone comes with a problem, we solve it, most of my clients continue towards personal growth and increased awareness. I started working to improve my life early. I can't tell you if it is because of the mess I grew up in, or if I have adapted a Kaizen attitude. Kaizen in the Japanese idea of constant improvement.*

I like Kaizen in my life. To me, it is the embodiment of getting in front of the suffering. Compassion leads to Kaizen, to being and doing better so no one suffers.

But we seem to learn through suffering and avoidance of suffering.

We can do better, we can avoid the pain and suffering in the first place and choose to learn through positive preemptive forethought.

Self-knowledge is not the realm of the weak. It is the realm of finding ourselves under what we think we are. It is the courage to face your own assumptions about yourself and the world with an objective eye. We are all saints in some areas and jerks in another. What if we had the courage, the strength in our souls to see through our own thoughts, our fear of self-judgment, and make conscious choices about how we treat ourselves and others? Right now too often, we are unconscious about this matter.

How can you contribute to seeing each other as humans instead of limiting the value of another to what they can do for you? What if we did not fear each other for the mundane differences we have, but looked with intelligence and compassion beyond the thin veil of thoughts that make up the egoic mask worn in public?

What if everyone had the courage to thrive through awareness and compassion? This is the root of many religious teachings, the reason behind the golden rule, and the only thing that will stop the decline of our mental, emotional, spiritual, financial, and political crisis. The ego that has taken hold of humans is self-destructing. Unless we have the courage to open our minds, hearts, and souls to what is deeper, we are all going to crash together and have to pick up the pieces.

We can choose advancement through compassion or suffering.

People often fear sounding like a victim if they talk about their problems. But talking about problems is done to resolve them, sometimes that means that we accept the problem and put our faith in the Creator asking inner wisdom to help us learn and grow through the issue or to stop suffering through acceptance.

Not sharing the challenges of life, doesn't make you strong, it makes you brittle, easily broken, resistant to others, it causes you to create inner mental/emotional states that fear feeds on.

I discourage victim mentality. I lived with it for years, and it nearly destroyed my life. Growing up I had a mess of a family. Despite a lot of counseling I still held that bitterness, the distrust, the victim inside of me. It contributed to my self-sabotage and unhappiness in relationships.

As you may have concluded by now I have faith in a Higher Power. Without that, I don't think I would have been able to go on in life.

What I had fought was the idea that things happen by our agreement or at least with a purpose that is meaningful to our soul and Higher Power even if I don't understand it, opposing it causes suffering. Things changed for me when learned that there is a real difference between acceptance of reality and resignation to victim identity. I thought my suffering had been in vain and could not imagine that I agreed to partake in the abuses that occurred for me as a child.

Let me be clear, I don't think that the Creator condones evil against children or abuse, but this evil happens, it hurts us, and we are more powerful than anything that happens to us. In finding our soul, wisdom, compassion, and humanity through these things, we are leaning on the good in the Creator instead of succumbing to the transitory effect of evil.

There are victims, and we all can truly say we are victims of something, but we also can overcome anything done to us by evil. And perhaps that is a lesson we can take away: that we are more than what we think, more than what happens to us, and more than anything we feel we need to hide. If you are hiding it, it is owning you.

One of the biggest problems with hiding our "bad" emotions is that it makes us mean towards others. It creates an inner dynamic of not trusting that comes out on the people around us. The root of many violent and mean people's behavior is that the pain and suffering living inside of them come out on those around them. Unattended to, our emotions are triggered time bombs that hurt us and those we love, and our teammates.

So now you can put aside images of group therapy and kumbaya. These are only for some people. Having a friend whom you agree to share honestly can be enough, a counselor, coach, or a book like this that gives you a place for inner exploration are all good tools. Some of us are private, and that is fine, just don't hide what lives and breeds in your heart, mind, body, emotions, spirit, and soul. I know one man who uses his walks to meditate and focuses on the bird feeder when he does his inner work. It works for him. Use your time on earth wisely, leave a mark that uplifts us all, don't carry around hate, fear, or negativity. This is not good for anyone. Any idea that you think is more important than life is evil.

If we become so individual as to neglect the whole or so self-avoidant as to work outside of ourselves without giving ourselves adequate care, we have lost the middle ground where our soul, our connection to the Creator, is found.

This is the presence that brings us to the Creator, our soul speaking to the Divine.

Compassion is seeing that each person is a valuable creation of the universe. We have the power to be respectful, one way to do this is to hold each person, including ourselves, in esteem; this reduces suffering. When you look at Maslow's Hierarchy of needs, you will see that survival is the first need that must be met before advancement or self-actualizing.

4

The tribe is key to human betterment, as is self-esteem. If the tribe denies its members esteem it continuously pulls its members into the pit of survival where the worse behavior is normalized as ideas of competition for resources, and stimulation of rampant fears, some are founded, most others are not.

No person is made to bend to our will, as we should not be bending to the will of others. Each interaction is an opportunity to create together, a chance to be successful in relating.

One of the powers of the Enneagram is that it reveals the motivation that each of us inherently believes will lead us to our personal connection with the eternal part of our being. The assumption being that our wholeness, or wellbeing is found in this connection.

You will notice when you read about the qualities of styles in survival mode, which is the lower functioning or stressed out state: that some people are blind to others' humanity, will pit themselves against others, dehumanize through judgment or self-aggrandization, some become self-forgetting, and still others numb out. Notice all styles have dysfunction that increases when they are in survival mode.

You will also notice that as a person is functioning at a higher level within their style, their behavior leaves the dysfunction of survival mode and moves into balanced behaviors that reflect compassion, care for the self, and consideration of others, acceptance, and recognition towards the needs of the whole. It is a balanced intelligence, that remains attentive to the present and respects the differences, strengths, similarities, and challenges all people face in the world. These are the bridges that make our world a better place to live.

As you look through the styles you will intuitively notice that each style holds value to contribute to the whole and that no one style is best or better.

To disregard or disrespect a person is dehumanizing. Most of the human conflict could be resolved with understanding, cooperation and mutual respect not with dismissing others or defending ourselves.

The Enneagram as a system has been contributed to by philosophers, teachers, and leaders in human psychology for centuries, and perhaps millennia. Giving it the power to transcend cultural barriers and to see the personality style of the culture, to consider its effects on the individuals of different styles within a social system.

It is my hope and intention that you use the information in the following pages to learn to see other people. Too much self-righteousness and positioning are causing great havoc in the world.

Of great importance is seeing yourself honestly and compassionately. We have been enculturated to not look too closely at ourselves, to associate blame with responsibility, and to think that the correction to a mistake as punishment instead of prevention. Think about the current system based on hindsight, blame, and punishment; when you say it out loud, it sounds like the insanity it is, but we fear change, so it goes on.

What if we learned to harness the power of our ability to choose so that we preemptively chose compassion and consideration towards everyone?

What if we gave ourselves a bit of time to learn about each other instead of dismissing what isn't like us? Come on, we can do this! It's in Dr. Seuss, we got it when we were 5! Then we lost it. We got lost in being more right than happy, more self-possessed than self-aware, more protective than willing to learn. Lost in fear that you will make mistakes and in thinking that we would get more if we competed instead of cooperated.

Building Bridges starts where you are. Small bridges, tall bridges, bridges that are in ports and bridges that are short; they all connect us to each other. Gives us the means to be happier, more productive, and healthier.

How Do I Use Personality Style Information?

➢ Read through all the styles.
- o We all have some of each style in us.
- o One style will emerge as "your" main style.

➢ Use the information to help you reflect on yourself.
- o You have light, dark, and neutral in you, you have to see this if you are ever going to advance.
- o The more you know about yourself better choices you can make. There is no hiding from yourself, but you have the power to reform yourself through your conscious choices.

➢ Think about the people around you.
- o They all have personalities that you interact with every day.
- o We all have some of every style in us, so we can relate at least a little to everyone.
- o Don't get too hung up on guessing the style of other people.
- o Notice the connection points and let those work for you.

➢ Look at for mutual qualities.
- o See where you can easily relate.
- o Consider your differences.
- o Pay attention and don't take the other's personality personally.
  - If a person's style is to withdraw, don't think it is because of something you've done.
  - People's behavior is about their experience.
  - Relationships will trigger emotions, we want to take personal responsibility for our actions and be compassionate.
  - Your responsibility is to consider them with forethought in your action. to do your best to communicate.

➢ You can make choices to solve problems before they happen.

➢ Educate yourself so you stop wasting precious time and start enjoying good relationships. That is what building bridges is about.

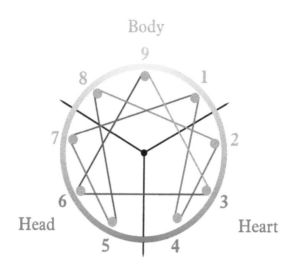

Perfectionist/ Reformer (1)

Helper/Giver (2)

Achiever/Performer (3)

Romantic/Individualist (4)

Intellectual/Investigator (5)

Loyal Skeptic (6)

Enthusiast/Epicure (7)

Challenger/Influencer (8)

Peacemaker/Mediator (9)

What is the Enneagram?

The Enneagram is a tool that provides you with valuable insight into the complex world of personalities, survival instincts, center, and human motivations.

The symbol is based on a circular image with 9 points, called styles.

Styles are a collection of personality traits that help us to see ourselves and others more clearly when we choose to use the information for self-awareness and behave more compassionately.

We can appear to have different personalities based on the environment we are in, for example, work vs home.

The Enneagram accounts for this in numerous ways.

1) Acknowledgment that we all have some of each style.
2) Wings and Arrows, which are influences from other styles. This is explained further on in the book.
3) Our survival instincts which are explained later.
4) Our culture or society in which we were raised. The cultural application is an advanced study not addressed in this work. A simple example is that entire nations or regions take on a personality style. This affects us, even though it is not really our style. This is true of family or any group that influences our thinking and behavior.
5) The fact is that humans are rather genius at surviving and adapt to a great number of situations as we need to for survival.

Of course, then we must come to the singular point of which style a person is. While you can take your behavior and weigh a vast number of factors to get to the "one" style, the true bottom line is what is your primary motivation in life? As you read through the personality styles you will notice motivation is an underlying factor.

9

Some say that our motivation is:

1) our attempt to balance what we feel is lacking or

2) the way we feel will find our connection to the Creator.

The reason we don't just start with the question of what motivates us is that most of the time, we are not 100% truthful with ourselves. Learning about the different qualities of the styles helps us to narrow things down; most importantly, to be very honest with ourselves.

You can gain a clear answer about their style by reading the material and having an assessment. Most people, couples, managers, and teams, benefit from working with a professional.

The system can be used simply to see yourself and others in a more compassionate light. More compassion because we all have value. Each person has highs/lows, strengths/stressors. None of us thrive in isolation, and we all react according to our nature. We can help each other, in doing so our lives are much better: more productive, creative, and our well-being increases.

It reminds us that we are all human. That we have many aspects, and that we are here to learn to respect our own and other people's nature. You see it is a complete circle, no point is superior, and all are connected. A reminder to assist rather than judge each other!

It expands our minds about other people.

Using the insights and tools provided, you can understand yourself and others, allowing you to make better choices for prosperous, purposeful and connected relationships.

About this book

A personal note, this book is one of my contributions to bringing balance to humanity and individual needs. If we look around us there are extremes in wealth and poverty, education, opportunity, food supply. There is also a devastating war between ideas and ideals that separate us.

Too many people are in their information echo chambers with their fist in the air, looking out for themselves and damning people who don't think like them. This is on both sides of the aisle, no one is innocent, but we all have the power to do something about it.

Individual rights are critical to our well-being and mental health, but so is a connection to a tribe, feeling our place in the world, with our family and workmates. Collective and group needs must be addressed, and unless we learn the critical lessons of allowing the individual to thrive within a supportive group, we all continue to suffer.

A person's religion, sexual identity, race etc. do not tell you anything about their character. I see people on all sides of the many current debates find fault with personal choices and expressions that are not our business. How a person behaves within the society is what matters, not if you like who they are. Regardless of personal ideas, we all have to work together.

It is not the place of the group to tell the individual who they should be, rather it is the responsibility of the whole to work together to create a safe space with respect for each other. I am talking about all human beings who are not harming others having equal humanity and rights. All must work together because we need the tribe to mature. Without the tribe we don't survive, without individual maturity we don't thrive.

The world is made up of nearly 7.5 billion people, we must learn to effectively relate to each other and work together to tame the chaos.

The key is finding the way we respect all aspects of our humanity.

Building Bridges is my answer; and since everyone has a personality, it's a great place to start building.

The business need for this book arose from using the Enneagram with my clients in busy workplaces. I found that there was interest, but the information needed to be presented in manageable sized chunks. Most of the Enneagram work I found was geared towards those with genius or at least strong interest in the fields of therapy, psychology, or coaching. In this book, the accompanying YouTube videos, and training manual, I have focused on making the information easily accessible to those who have not trained in the language of the therapist.

I have used both narrative and bullet points to help you develop a working knowledge of the system.

Some people have little time to study the softer skills, the emotional intelligence necessary for success. Yet, we all know that people need each other in all areas of life. It is through relationships that many projects, companies, and all forms of partnership are built or crumble. Sometimes having a quick way to remember details about personality helps us to navigate the waters with more ease.

This book and the additional tools are designed for you to be able to contemplate on one page, read a section, reference a certain type, or to read it from cover to cover. If you want to understand yourself or another person, you can go to the sections that relate to them.

Much of the work on the Enneagram is quite clinical, deeply thought through and can feel a bit overwhelming to people who have their skills and training in other areas. As with everything, the deeper you go into the subject, the more the nuances and contradictions show up.

I attempted to remember what I needed at the beginning of my Enneagram studies and drew from the questions of my clients in compiling the information in this book.

Look at my YouTube channel for videos that help bring the styles to life and go deeper into specific topics. Send a question and I will create a video.

YouTube: Naomi Eklund or Infinite Yes Productions

If you have purchased the book, please email me at the office for a series of downloadable charts.

naomi@infiniteyesinc.com

There is a training manual for companies available. At the time of this writing, a series of online videos are being developed to increase accessibility and reduce training cost.

You can reach me for Coaching and Training at:

www.infiniteyesinc.com

Speaking engagements, I am a graduate of the National Speakers Association Academy, currently volunteering with Speakers Academy, facilitating National Speakers Association, Oregon - Speakers Labs, and have been speaking publicly for 35 years. I am happy to tailor my presentation to your group's needs. Group discounts are available for books and services.

If you would like to carry this book in your shop, have me speak to your group or to learn more about partnering for relationship (teamwork) success you can reach my office at:

Naomi@infiniteyesinc.com

The Whisper that Leads Us to Greatness.

Is it put there by our Creator? Our hearts?

An ember of something bigger than our own life lingering and calling to us, it promises fulfillment. It is within us, but we hide from it in the chores, the inbox, the lawn, or the game.

These distractions can quiet the whisper... sort of.

When I worked elder care no one ever revealed that they wished they had watched more tv, kept a cleaner house or squeezed an extra ounce out of their staff. Often there were more poignant confessions... I wish I had... but I didn't, think I could have, I always wanted to, it wasn't allowed or practical. I never found time to...

I wish I would have... been courageous!

Our whisper, that longs for life, is fed by courage.

It may be outrageous or impractical to others,

But it's our dream, hope, longing, responsibility.

You can support or sabotage the whisper that is inseparable from your soul.

There is no success without changing choices. There is no change or wisdom without knowledge. Are you willing to understand yourself?

To use self-knowledge to increase self-love: to make choices that change the course of your life?

Use this information as a mirror, to see yourself, to find hidden gems and nourish them.

14

Find gems in those around you and have the strength to say yes to the whispers of another's soul as you do your own.

Love is courageous.

Compassion is courageous.

Self-knowledge is a radical disruption of the dysfunction that we trudge through.

Good Leadership is courageous.

We live in a world that aches for disruption.

Acts of courage give us faith in life.

Acts of courage make life rich.

Today you are challenged as A human

A leader

A manager

A parent

A partner

A friend

To find what is true in you and about you, to take this and bring it to the world as a conscious choice.

Find what is whispering inside of you and bring it to life, now!

There is no time to lose.

Using the Information in this Book

➤ You can start from the front to the back and study the overall system.
➤ Use the information to understand yourself, and those around you.
➤ Look for exercises or guidance within the sections.
➤ Use the information to recognize the sameness and differences in each person.
➤ Think about ways to connect with people of different types.
➤ This is the first book in the series. It is meant to create a foundation of information.
➤ You can use the sections to look up information as you need it.
➤ Refresh your knowledge as needed.
➤ The more you understand yourself and others, the easier it is to get along, enjoy life and be productive.
➤ Use this information to be more objective about your interactions and consider the needs of yourself and others.
➤ Understand the elements that make up personalities. This is a great advantage in a world made up of people who are using their personality in every interaction.
➤ Remember personalities are structures we create to get along in the world. Compassion and understanding with ourselves and each other bring success to our common goals.
➤ Understand your highs and lows, if you are not in a good place, take some action to improve your state.
➤ Give yourself and others grace, things you judge yourself for are likely things that you can improve by looking at yourself or another with a new point of view.

Building Bridges

Bridges create economies, bring together islands, make expansion possible, they are extremely useful. Imagine Chicago, London, Hong Kong, China, or Cairo without bridges. Stop and think of the great cities on all continents, they all have bridges!

They are beautiful, useful, and made by humans to purposefully connect. Perhaps among our greatest architectural and cultural achievements. They work for all people, of any race, any gender, and all belief systems.

Imagine a world where we intentionally built bridges with each other. We could hold our own space and meet on a bridge to see the vast expanse of possibilities where all of us brought our differences and similarities to create together a cooperative productive consciously connected reality in which we have a greater chance to thrive, be healed, be happy, contribute.

As individuals, we are designed to create a personal world based on our thoughts, feelings, experiences, motivations, needs, and interpretations of events. Yet from within this world, we must create a common experience. To have a tribe, a culture, a place in the world that is much more than an individual. We need each other to get anything done. Building Bridges is the way that we can share ourselves without destroying our own world or having to argue with someone else about theirs. Knowing about different personality styles is a way to build those bridges, to not take things personally and to have insight into the way others experience the world.

19

Since we all develop our different personalities through the same natural internal process, and all must share the planet, we might infer, that like a forest ecosystem, we are meant to learn to work together. That we are beings of our own perception and of the world around us. That we are inseparable from the reality of our connection, as equally as we are beings created by our own perception.

Bridges are a logical answer to this dilemma:

- ➤ They allow us to have our personal worlds,
- ➤ To understand through our unique perception,
- ➤ To find the connection points where we can build a relationship.
- ➤ We meet on the bridge to view the landscape, to find our way together and help each other individually through the landscape.

We travel through life as individuals together. We all strive to survive. The damage comes when we believe that our survival is threatened by another. It is rare that another person threatens our lives.

Other's thriving generally does not take away from our own ability to thrive. The confusing part is where do we fit into the whole? Where are we responsible for each other's survival as well as our own?

This can pit us against our fellow humans and cause mass destruction, loss of creativity, pain, suffering and the collective consciousness that dehumanizes others, especially if they don't think as we do. You can't harm someone until they are dehumanized in your eyes. If you are putting people down, shunning them, ridiculing them, you are dehumanizing them; putting a hard spot on your heart and in your mind, that allows you to mistreat another person.

Meeting on the bridges that we create, our own world is intact. We need personal boundaries, but not brick walls. We need to see that we are safe even when ideas are different. New ideas are not a threat, seeing another person as a human is not a threat, learning from each other is not a threat. We don't have to agree with each other, but we must accept their rights re equal to ours. People need to be given space and attention, we must learn to care about them, not see them simply as a sum of our ideas about their ideas. It behooves us all to find the commonality that binds us.

The only way to expand our world, to include change and not feel threatened is to build a bridge where we can meet with others and hear them/be heard. In the best cases, you find places to agree and co-create, to strategize for productive prosperous outcomes, and happy relationships. We can humanize ourselves and each other, practice compassion, be better people and become more productive and happier.

At the writing of this, our news shows us in very dire straits. Everyone is shouting and few are listening. This is true in too many ways. Yet, I meet many people who are learning to listen, opening their world, finding ways to explore the larger playing field of life.

You will never change a person's mind by yelling at them, by telling them that they are wrong, or by taking the stance that only you are right. If you believe in a higher power at all, there are endless equalizers, saying to us, that we must learn to work together. That means, finding even the most basic threads and use those to build a bridge. A few things we all want or need is to eat, to be housed, to have good chances for our kids, to enjoy our work, to feel appreciated for our contributions, to be seen, to contribute to the success of our team.

None of us, want to be dehumanized. If you are dealing with a "troubled" person, there is a good chance that they have been dehumanized. None of us want to feel we are invalidated as a human being. Since we all identify with the world we built and live in, changing our thoughts to agree with or accommodate others feels potentially dangerous. Therefore, I suggest we recognize each other's worlds and meet on a bridge of respect, working to understand and provide a workable place for all concerned.

Sometimes you are dealing with a person who wants to stay in their position. You are not the one to "fix" others, and if you meet a toxic person, you have to do your best to:

> 1) Apply the golden rule to yourself. How do you want to treat yourself? Keeping in mind that you are the only one you control. You won't be able to make them treat you a certain way if they don't want to. So, decide who you want to be in the situation, while you do not allow them to harm you. If you are their manager, go to HR, implement good strategies for your whole team, and don't allow a bully to take root on your team.

> 2) Apply the golden rule to those around you. You are who you choose to be, your actions reflect your choices. How people respond is not in your control: DON'T TAKE OTHER PEOPLE'S BEHAVIOR PERSONALLY!

This may seem a bit contradictory because I am saying don't take their behavior personally but do take a personal interest in how you treat them.

It is easy: do your best with compassion to humanize each other consider them in your behavior equation. But don't expect that you are in control of their reaction. If there is a conversation or a need for one, don't fear it. Don't fear feelings and do look for places that you are able to build bridges toward an agreement.

If we all choose to meet each other on the bridge, in a safe place to exchange ideas, develop "good trades" of respect and insight into each other's worlds, our natural sense of compassion can help us to learn, to expand our understanding of life, easing our fears.

Through compassion and intelligence or war and violence, we will learn that our survival depends on each other. No one style of person is going to win. That is not the way of things. All styles have purpose and value to contribute.

We are here to work together, to find how the differences make a team, a family, or a friendship strong. Don't get me wrong there are relationships that have to end, this too is the nature of things. But each one of us has something to contribute. When we hold our own mirror up to find our best self and choose to see each other's best self, this is the point on the bridge where we are better people. Where everybody wins.

Imagine your team, if everyone knew their best self, saw each other as allies and consciously chose to work together towards the team goals in their strengths! Imagine yourself as the manager, leader, friend or family member who helps make this a reality.

It is challenging to learn for most adults, we become set in our ways. The brain has a mechanism to "not deplete itself" or conserve energy, which makes vegging out very popular. We must be careful about giving up our right to choose our identity to the makers of the TV shows that we veg out to, and find the value in challenging ourselves, so the brain feels it is worth the effort to learn new things that improve our lives and the world in which we live.

Having fun with the Enneagram helps people to engage. I also use improv as a training tool because it's fun. The foundation of improv is "Yes AND…" Never make your teammates or the other person wrong. Hear them! Find ways that your points of view are complementary: Notice how the Yes AND lives in the following scenario. Of course, people are capable of many things and never should be limited by their style description.

A Challenger/Influencer, who leads the division might say: "we have to gather our forces to get this product offer together. Our Sales team needs us, so they can bring home the mammoth".

The Helper/Giver might say: Hmmm, I know three folks at the company we are pitching to and the former HR director. "Let me get on the phone and connect with them, gathering intel to help my team."

The Achiever/Performer is going to see the needed result and help from the presentation.

The Romantic/Individualist is going to look for the ways to craft the offer that highlights the emotionally appealing factors and woo the client.

The Intellectual/Investigator will jump into action, making sure the product offering is up to date legally and that you have the best most detailed and accurate information.

The Loyal Skeptic might intentionally bring in some humor to help equalize the situation. This person is going to analyze your client's needs, your services, and all the intel from the Helper/Giver. They are going to ask tough questions, so you have the answers before your client needs them.

The Enthusiast/Epicure keeps the team energized and finds angles that illuminate how awesome your product is, often being able to see a futurist vision and helping to craft the offer accordingly.

The Peacemaker/Mediator will assure that the job is going smoothly, that everyone is working well, and may find themselves filling the gaps for people, buoying up the team.

The Perfectionist/Reformer is going to deliver the most perfect work they can and will likely have an overall vision for the project that they are willing to sacrifice for, they will find great personal dedication to bring their vision to reality.

Notice that this project is likely to be successful with all these various points of view working towards a common goal.

Look at the power of diversity. It gives you a good idea of why having a team with many styles will give you a better outcome. BIG mistakes people make when hiring is: hiring people who are too much like themselves, who will fit in, who they will relate to. While there must be some mutuality and capability, you need to step back and think about the value of different personalities on a team. What you need to be successful in the ever-increasing competitive world that is full of diversity, not homogeny.

Diversity does not have to mean conflict, it means that everyone on the team must stand up and challenge themselves to open minds and hearts. If you consider this: As a leader, you are obligated to build a team that provides the company with the best outcome. You are not obligated to make everyone happy, yet you must have them all work together.

Sometimes you must carry the burden of leadership and lead them into better behavior. It is on your shoulders to say: we are going to learn about each other and round out our teams. To expand our point of view so that we can all do better. It is on you to set a cultural standard, to model the Yes AND or slide back into an underdeveloped state that leads to a monotonous, stagnant culture, that suffers from drama and brain drain.

To grow you need knowledge so you can improve your choices and guide wisely how things can change.

As parents, spouses, and partners, it is up to you to learn about the ways you and your loved ones are alike and different and to not take their nature personally.

Parenting is tough. You have to find a way to build a good character and give the individual a chance to grow into themselves. Not to tell them who they are, but to create a standard of character that makes them healthy, contributing citizens, and we hope happy adults.

What is the best personality style for me to be in a relationship with?

Any style that is healthy or willing to work at it!

There is no perfect couple's combo. There are some natural fits that I have observed, but it always comes down to how willing are all members to:

> ➤ become self-aware.
> ➤ take personal responsibility for their mental, emotional, physical and spiritual condition.
> > o How compatible are you in your approaches to these?
> ➤ consider the way their thoughts, actions, behaviors, needs, wants, and beliefs influence the other person.
> ➤ learn about each other.
> ➤ be genuine with yourself and your partner about your needs.
> ➤ hear different opinions and consider that it does not matter if you agree or not. It is natural and healthy to have different needs, wants, and opinions.
> ➤ If someone never needs anything, this is a warning sign.

> ➤ Among the biggest challenges I see in relationships is that in the courting phase people want love so badly they put themselves to the side or agree to what the other says without really considering it as an ideal that they will have to live with for the length of the relationship. When they become disenchanted with this, things fall apart.
> ➤ Also, people feel threatened when they don't agree with the people, they are closest to. This has to do with letting your identity be built by the world around us rather than making a conscious, self-aware decision. You don't have to agree to be in love, you should not define each other, and you will be a stronger smarter person if you allow your loved ones their opinions, needs etc.

- If someone agrees too much, that is a warning sign.
- Use the Enneagram as a talking point to expand your understanding of each other.
- There are toxic people out there, and bad fits, you need to get free of these.
- Long-term relationships can require more of you than you imagine until you are already in it. Yet, they can be worth the work if you develop a love for each other and are willing to work on it together.
- The point of relationships can be more than need fulfillment. It can be upliftment, esteem, purpose and accomplishing things in life together whether it's raising a building, a product, or a family.
- The point of having good relationships is to experience support, advancement, opportunity, cooperation, and love.
  - To have a helpmate in the world.
  - To build together.
  - To have a friend that has your back. You are a better friend, lover, partner if you know yourself and each other accepting the easy places and being grateful for the places where we help each other grow.

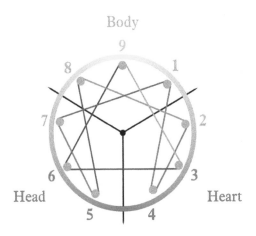

Body
9

8   1

7   2

6   3
Head   Heart
5   4

About the Enneagram

Ennea means 9

Gram means picture

9 is a number that represents the completion of the cycle of the first 10 numbers, zero is a place holder. The Enneagram is a circle with a picture of 9 points. Each one represents a group of behaviors, and most importantly a primary drive or motivation. The drive is what we feel will complete us or get us to happiness. It is what we deeply believe will get us to our souls, and perhaps to connect us to our Creator.

In 18 years of study, I have grown to love the Enneagram. It can be used simply or in depth. Used by people of all walks of life, faiths, or absences of faith, by those in business, and by families.

This is because it is about seeing the elements and potential of each person. It expands our understanding by seeing that all people have all elements of personality in them and some are more profoundly present than others.

The Enneagram is reported to be progressively built upon by scholars and philosophers from the past 2,000 years. I believe that the underlying

29

integration of the soul into its teachings gives it strength and humanity that is not often found in "personality typing systems". Also, having had so much input helps it to be a translatable system. One that adapts to the common language and can serve people at many levels of education and across cultures. You can use it according to your abilities, education, and needs.

In most writings on the Enneagram, you will find that the numbers are referred to as a shorthand. In this book, especially as it is meant to give you a base of understanding rather than to be an advanced work, I work to use the common names of the styles along with the numbers. I want to thank a client, Ron Safarik, VP of Participant Services, with Fringe Benefits Group of Austin, TX, for his feedback on the importance of "not creating an exclusive language" when using the system. While this thought had crossed my mind, I didn't act until he spoke up about it. I appreciate him crystalizing the thought into a comment. I agree with him. You don't need or want to use a new or exclusive language to get benefit from this work.

A Few Reasons the Enneagram Works:
1) It is humanistic.
2) Includes the soul, our drive and desire for divine connection in its point of view on people.
   a. I can't imagine that any healing can happen in a vacuum without the acknowledgment of the human need and drive for connection with our Creator. In fact, in all my years, I have found no healing without some form of spiritual awakening/awareness.
      i. It is interesting that science-minded people are also looking for answers to the mysteries of life and the universe. Some are looking for answers, some are looking for comfort in the proof of the why and how of the world. It is a mistake to say that people who are not religious are rejecting the Creator.

      ii. Any person should be related to through their character, never through your assumptions about them. Your assumptions are based on your thoughts, experiences emotions, which is different than theirs. Too much pain comes from misunderstandings that arise in this method.

   b. Connecting with the Creator is not necessarily in a religious context. In fact, if your experience with religions is negative, it might be more of a confidence in your soul and find what you need to feel in contact with the Creator.

3) Purpose is written about in so many places. I believe our purpose is to grow, expand, improve, to do our best to contribute to the advancement and wellbeing of humanity in an often chaotic world.

   a. The Enneagram supports us to find and express our purpose. It explains traits we have, revealing secrets we might hide from ourselves. It's a powerful mirror.

4) The system gives us information about our connection to others' personalities in a way that guides us through the maze of our lives, providing some reflection and direction to see ourselves and help us make our choices.

5) It helps us to be compassionate with ourselves. This helps us to stop with the judgment. Enabling us to see and use our strengths, giving us tools to improve and overcome our challenge areas instead of thinking you are supposed to be all things and get it right all the time.

Head/Heart/Body

You will notice that the words head, heart, and body appear around the outside number of the diagram.

This is one of the methods of grouping the Enneagram styles. These groups showing a significant similarity in styles that tells us how they process information.

I explained this briefly later in the book. What you need to know in a general sense is:

> We all have all three centers. One of the centers will be more prevalent or dominant in our experience and expression.
> Head people tend to lead with thinking
> Heart people to tend to lead with emotion
> Body people lead with instinct.
> Ideally, we all learn to balance and use all of the centers, yet, one will remain dominant.

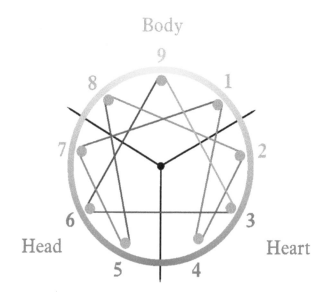

Why Relationships

I choose to focus this book series on relationships, because to me, people have always been beautiful, amazing and what I desire to understand. It is my nature to make things better for those I care about or anyone who will let me help.

I see relationships as bridges we choose to build between our worlds and other people's. Where my world exists on its own, and yours exist for you, we choose to expand our minds to find a point on a bridge where we meet. We share parts of our world, and that is what I mean by meeting on the bridge, in a safe place.

The richness in life comes in the sharing of our worlds. There are parts we keep to ourselves, and we share different parts with different people. This expands our world, gives us challenges to face, and support from those who love us or on our team.

Relationships transcend political and economic models, race, gender, and our wounds and triggers. Relationships are largely how we heal, and how we get hurt. They are certainly how we get things done. Isolation is the worse sort of condition. Don't get me wrong, good alone time is important and wonderful, but when we feel cut off from love, care, and human connection it is a mentally, emotionally dangerous state of being.

People and human connection are my passion. Everything is a relationship. Our relationship with our self starts when we look in the mirror and extends to our finances, our home, health, and everyone we meet or interact with in any way. It is internal and external, but it starts inside.

Personal Note: It was in my first college-level abnormal psychology class that the light bulb went on: I was right, my family was completely messed up.

33

I was a friendly, bright, connecting person. Truly loved people and would bend over backward for those I cared about. Don't get me wrong, I was also strong headed, strong-willed, can be sarcastic, contrary, and have a fierce sense of independence that may not always serve me well. But I was right that our family was a mess and not normal or healthy. That my efforts to improve were founded in good logic, but not well received. My sister finally explained that I was the only one who wanted to fix the family, everyone else just wanted out.

I was rather exquisitely broken by the abuse and neglect, along with the abandonment issues of a child adopted in the 1960s into a mentally unhealthy home.

I say exquisitely because I was conscious of having been broken. I think that was helpful. Without knowing it I was traveling along a path that is referred to as The Wounded Healer. There is a book by this name you can easily find.

This idea comes from a school of thought that says our wounds are not for nothing. That while the Divine does not will these upon us, these wounds can be used to heal others. Perhaps most importantly to put the "things of this world" in their place and pay attention to the whole of who and what we are, to find the soul, because that is the eternal part of us, while our wounds and successes only live if we keep them alive.

We can use our wounds, turn that into our genius, together we learn from and teach each other to heal and become better people.

My interest in people had always been there, it drove me to learn as much as I could about people, how to help them, how to develop and heal ourselves.

One of the reasons I was interested in people, was that I could see things others could not see. I could see their angels or guardians, their fear and hurts. I didn't always pay attention because most people don't want you

34

to see things about them that they are unaware of. I have had to condition myself over time to "not see".

I have mostly kept things to myself, the time I told someone, I lost a friend:

I was 12 and working with my parents' permission at a local diner for $1 an hour washing dishes. I really liked the cook. I don't remember her name, but a sweet blonde lady who let me help her cook and spoke kindly.

One day she walked in, tired, upset and trying to pull herself together for work. I sat down to comfort her at the back table where employees ate. I put my hand on her arm and saw the picture of what happened.

> *She was sitting in the hall; the bathroom light was on her. She was crying and then he came walking down the hall with his fist clenching.*

I was shocked that a grown woman would put up with this. In our house you could beat the kids, but not the mom! I looked at her and said, "why don't you tell him to stop. He shouldn't be hitting you. If he doesn't stop, you should leave".

Her face went into a blank horror. "How do you know that? You don't understand". She pulled away from me and our friendship was not the same – ever again.

That is how I learned to stop telling people what I saw, also the moment I was certain the way I saw the world was weird. It drove me into psychology so I would be able to help them without letting them know how much I can see intuitively.

This gave me tangible reference points to explain my intuition and tools to create the bridges with people that I needed to be genuinely helpful. It brought my spiritual knowing and science together. It was smarter and safer for all concerned and helped me to sort out thoughts and feelings to provide an objective point of view.

Being an empath, I can feel others' feelings. It is not always easy to separate my feelings from other people's. My studies have helped me to create boundaries and sort out what was once an overwhelming amount of emotional and energetic input from others and the world around me.

Being very empathetic is hard in relationships. The natural drive to feel and be closely connected can lead people like me to take on too much of what is truly other people's and miss what is mine. You might be able to conclude that understanding people and relationships served many purposes in my life, including how to manage in the world.

The Enneagram has helped me a great deal on this quest to cope, function, and thrive in the world.

Always being a fan of self-help workshops:

When my son was 3 and I was looking down the long barrel of a divorce, one of my friends, said, "let's go to this seminar".

It was my weekend "off", there were few of those. I needed to get away and learning something at this retreat center sounded like heaven.

In the first half of the first day, the course of my life changed. Oh, I wish I could say something lovely here, but the truth is the seminar leader "diagnosed" me with a personality style. The "worst" personality style for a woman (in his opinion) and clearly, he judged me for it. So, yes, my life changed because I was so angry at his answer. I had felt publicly put down and rejected.

I was getting divorced. I was in emotional turmoil. He said in a belittling tone that I was an 8. This is the angry, problematic, type (per his description). Completely ignoring the rest of me, he rejected all the reasons I thought I might be different styles. Worse he said nothing to help me see the "good stuff". This added to the sorrow I was in because I had not learned about the upside and the tools to move along the path from angry to loving (surviving to thriving).

36

Not being a quitter and wanting to prove him wrong. I set about learning as much as I could about all the types and trying on all the styles that seemed possible. It was an enormous endeavor and took many years to get clear on.

In the process I learned more than I ever imagined possible about the Enneagram, and what it is like to live in different styles. In my efforts to determine my final answer, I walked through the different styles, learning them as if they were mine. I lived thinking I was that style. One of my favorite practices was to take qualities of the style and meditate in that quality for a long time.

This gave me a chance to really get a feeling of what it was like to be a **Romantic/Individualist (style 4)** riding the waves of emotion into places that most people dare not tread. Standing in the emotional storms of life with a sort of courage that few can demonstrate in this world. But then also feeling the distress of the mundane. The death that arises when too much average is taking over. And the sort of foggy hypnosis called a trance that I used to avoid the mind-numbing unpleasantness of reality. I found my inner rebel, "they don't define me", pushing me not to conform. Literally experiencing the distaste of conformity, and the irritating reality that I have to conform to some degree to survive.

I lived in the "checked out" mental mist of the stressed-out **Peacemaker/Mediator (style 9)**. People pleasing and numbing out so that I could avoid conflict. Later to find the amazing strength and objectivity that is available on the upside of this style. I found myself going inward further than ever before to gather my resources, to find a peaceful escape from the world. I also gained insight into seeing all sides of a story, feeling a strong desire to have everyone treated fairly. What surprised me most was the well of passionate resentment for the demands that the world put on me that stole my peace.

It is amazing to put yourself in the deeply analytical place of the **Loyal Skeptic, (style 6)**. To see and feel the endless streams of information that go into deciding who and what is worthy of your faith and loyalty. Then to experience the passionate drive the faith inside sparks. This was a tough one for me, because of fear, anxiety was not something that I could make myself "at home with". It was pretty clear to me early into the experience that I was not a Loyal Skeptic, but I am glad for what I could learn intentionally putting myself in their place.

It was shocking to me to see that in some areas of my life, I was much more of a **Perfectionist/Reformer (style 1)** than I would have ever guessed. The further revelation was that I was guilty of so much judgment on myself and others. My ability to have a vision for my life and hope for humanity had become more of a right/wrong thing in my mind than an inspiring vision to share. The best part of diving into my experience in the shoes of the Perfectionist/Reformer (1) experience was to allow myself to find God in executing the well-done. Not delegating was hard but there was some satisfaction of getting things done just the way I saw it in my head.

I indulged the idea that I might be an **Enthusiast/Epicure (style 7)**, for a short while. But I really don't have the right constitution for it. I am not the most fun person in the room, I am more into the work of things. But I can relate to the experience of saying yes to the fun, of wanting to be where the fun is, loving new experiences, and of taking on too much.

Living as a **Helper/Giver (style2)** was eye-opening. This is related to my actual Challenger/Influencer (style 8). So it felt almost like home but I really wasn't completely comfortable. I found it more difficult than what most Helper/Givers (2) say they do to consume myself with others' needs. Also, the demands on appearance were hard for me. I am much more of a Challenger/Influencer (8) in my appearance and could not bring myself to the fine level of detail I see in most Helper/Giver's (2) appearance. I definitely dress for myself, while as a Helper said to me once: "I have to keep myself looking nice so people can be instantly comfortable with me, o let them know I care and can relate to whatever reason they might need me."

enjoy the cave of the **Intellectual/Investigator (style 5)**. This was my refuge as a young girl when I hid out in the library. It was my favorite haven from a chaotic world. There is something live affirming and energizing about reading and experiencing what I was through the written words, as if it were real, maybe more real than the crassness of those too lazy to educate themselves or too needy to stand on their own.

There are endless worlds to enjoy, knowledge to be found and few people to intrude on my sacred world. In my meditations on this style, I was able to tap into just how miserable and draining people feel to the Intellectual. It was hard to imagine but it's almost like a disdain for ignorance, a chalky taste that others lack of mental effort leaves on their palate.

Because I am passionate about my work, I thought I might be an **Achiever/Performer (style 3)**. I quickly put that notion aside. I am far too non-conformist to be an Achiever/Performer (3) and far too cavalier about my wardrobe. Before this exercise, I judged the Achiever as cold and inhuman. What I found is this compulsiveness towards doing can be fun but can also push away your loved ones. Also, it's a burden to always be on.

Finally, I came back home to be a **Challenger/Influencer, (style 8)** with a whole new point of view. Landing in my own style was finally comfortable. I learned truly that we all have all styles in us, that we can learn to access those gifts and talents, and that when you land in your primary style and see the way it fits, it's a relief. I had to learn that Power was not a bad thing, though it can be used that way.

Trying on all these styles over a course of years gave me insight and empathy for each type but also, showed me that all styles have ups and downs. The thing is, that when you land in the place that feels like home, you have found your style.

Our teachers make such a difference as illustrated in the above story. I want to thank Dale Rhodes M.S, M.A., who over several years led workshops and private sessions in which I polished and honed my love of the Enneagram, and finally landed in my style.

A big Thank you to Tom Condon, a leader in the Enneagram field for over 30 years. In his workshops and our private sessions, his clear head, a light heart, and command of the Enneagram helped me move into this graceful knowing of the system. These two wonderful men have blessed my path as teachers.

Also, to my dear soul friend Gabriele. We talked for many hours of the Enneagram and life. Her passion fueled my interest and knowledge. I continue to cherish her in so many ways. She has the strength of an army when it comes to discovery and self-knowledge. She is truly an inspiration.

Our friends are sometimes our best teachers as they share our lives. I am blessed with great friends, and another soul sister who must be acknowledged here in my Enneagram thank you list is Rosie. She is always upfront and it was her advice that the book needed more narrative. This helped me to reform my vision and execution. To all of my friends who encouraged and celebrate this book coming into being – thank you!

Thank you to my clients for their trust in my coaching. Those who over the years have worked with me as we took the system, proved its validity and saw a real change in people's understanding of themselves, in managers interactions with their teams and in leaders stepping into their roles with more success, strength, and compassion.

I celebrate being a Challenger of the status quo, An Influencer whose power is based in Love, a boss of an empire built on inspiration, and giving my power to increase compassion and improve relationships in the world. I am an 8, a woman 8, who has nothing to apologize for because I am finally accepting how I was made to be.

As a business owner: Understanding myself has been key to success. Self-awareness has given me a great drive. Knowing that I am not harming anyone and can do some good in the world, is such an empowering feeling, and seeing my own "stuff" has helped me to make sure that I am not sabotaging myself. Also, no one can send me a curveball, and if they do, I am more capable than ever of handling it.

As a natural Leader: I am programmed to NOT show my vulnerability, to judge this human part of me as a weakness. But, if I hold onto that belief, I am shut down. AND, like it or not people can see our weaknesses, our fears, and triggers. Think about how much you intuitively know. The way body language, facial expressions and the language people use betrays the competition. Consider people's tells that we read to get the upper hand in business or gather more information in your relationships. Well, others are reading you. If you don't know yourself, you are giving them the keys to your psychological, emotional kingdom.

As a Manager of people: Your staff has your number. They must because you represent survival. You control part of their life, have control over their quality of life at work, and affect their survival through wages and continued employment. If you don't look at yourself, you are missing out. They are much more aware of you than you may realize. Your job is to bring out the best in them. To help them perform for the company and feel good about their work life. It's a big job, and most people do this job with blinders, believing the staff will join them in the world the "boss" creates. How can you create an effective workplace if you aren't looking into the motivation and needs of the people you are charged with leading to success?

As a Parent: You are faced with the tough job of raising a whole human being. A person who will hopefully be a part of your whole life, and yet to do your job right you have to help them grow into their own best life. You must know about them and yourself so you can put your attention on balancing the struggles and co-creating the best life your child can have. You have to help them know themselves so they can make the best possible choices.

As a Partner or Spouse: You must have each other's backs. To help them be their healthiest self. You promise to know them, to care, to help each other and meet each other's needs. Also, to enjoy life together. Imagine having a cheat sheet of their personality style, what might be going on in their head or heart. If you want to be close to someone, getting to know their ups and downs helps you to know how to let go of things that you used to take personally, and to hold their hand as you both walk through life, doing your best to find purpose, love, and happiness.

Do not diagnose

Don't worry, you will guess at other people's styles. You may get it right, sometimes it is easy to see. But don't tell people what they are, ASK them! Never disagree with them about what they think their style is. If they ask you for feedback, you could say:

"I observe a lot of xyz qualities when you are working".

It is normal to have influences from our families, our culture, etc. show up in our personality. As you self-assess, step back, try to see what has been conditioned into you, or is that really you? Is that your parent or environment showing up in your life, or is that genuinely you?

Normally people will exhibit different qualities in their home vs work life, but the basic personality is still there. The thing that drives you towards your own connection with your soul, is always there.

I have taken the qualities of each personality style and put them into short narratives, bullet points, and charts that are easy to glance at, to compare and to use as a reflective tool. You will have some qualities of all the types, but a few will stand out.

To understand yourself within the Enneagram, you must understand your style. The singular defining question is what motivates you?

As a manager, having a formal assessment of your team members and a quick to reference Organizational chart can save you time and energy in communication with the team. I started doing this for clients years back and it is one of the handiest tools they have. This transcends many of the communication tools you are given because people will respond based on their style. People are not formulas, but they do have style!

Personality is Complex

Each person has many aspects:

> Instincts for survival
> Extrovert/Introvert/Ambivert
> Main Style
>> o Personal needs, drives, experiences, environmental influences.
> Wings, which of the styles next to your main style do you use, and when?
> Arrows, natural tendencies we express, and resources we can use to balance ourselves.
> Subtypes perhaps explained by our response to our parents.
> Other aspects not being covered here.

The Enneagram has been developed over many centuries, contributed to by many cultures, philosophies, as well as, religions. In my opinion, this makes it an outstanding, expanding, not limiting, assessment of personality styles.

It is valuable to have a tool that explains us to ourselves and helps us see others. We all have all types in our personalities, the assessment shows us where we operate most often.

Humans build worlds around their thoughts, feelings, and experience of "reality". We each have a world, our personality is the way we show ourselves to the world. It is a representation, some would say a hologram that we project into the world that represents us-a collection of the ideas about ourselves-but it is not the whole of us. A vehicle through which we relate and perceive information. This means that while there is a communal reality that we share, most people are more familiar with the world that they built to live in.

45

Reality is researched with attempts at explanations by scientist, by mystics, and by philosophers. What's real:

> Some say we are living a dream.
> Many lives happening at the same time, as is suggested by String Theory?
> Do we have past lives, personal, family, or cultural karma?
> Is there a place that is Heaven or Hell, or are these states of consciousness vs locations– or just dead when we are dead?
> Reincarnation? Limbo? Ghosts?
> Does our thought create our world or explain it?
> Endless possible explorations of these ideas…lead us to endless views and experiences of the world.

How you are brought up will form you. It will influence your thoughts, personality, and feelings about the world. As we are not brought up the same and don't all have the same personalities, we will find ourselves at odds with each other if we try to establish our own rightness and others wrongness.

In our attempts to tame the chaos around us and find our mutual experience of reality we have to find points that we can define and agree on: we say the sky is blue and water is wet because it's easier to create a baseline to relate through.

We all, as humans have basic needs. If those needs are not met, then we all suffer, become afraid and usually go into stressed states that reduce our capacity to perform and contribute. This is true for all races, all communities, across languages and cultures.

If you look at the basics of the human experience, there are lots of commonalities. Many points within reality where building bridges gives us support, encouraging us, providing resilience, and making our lives easier when we learn and work together.

Agreements are the key to good relating and knowledge is the key to good agreements. We can even agree to challenge each other to learn more or explore. Agreements can be dynamic and stimulating if we agree to go exploring together.

To reach agreement: we must understand what we share, look towards a goal that matters to us, define our rolls, consider our purpose, find ways that we contribute to the outcome and find our way through so many factors. Agreements reached with poor knowledge don't succeed. Therefore, the study of personality matters to our success.

The foundation of an agreement is knowledge, and if we don't consider the very doorways through which agreements are reached and executed how can we have successful relationships.

In this book, I am giving you insight for using the different personality information and introducing you to different elements involved in personalities that you will encounter every day.

If you simply read this book, you will get a good high-level view of the basic elements of people around you.

If you want to be a better leader, manager, partner or parent, to have better relationships in all areas of your life, you will put in the work to learn about other people and styles.

Be Preemptively Smart!

- ➢ Relationships struggle when people don't "get" each other. The tools of the Enneagram help us to increase our emotional intelligence:
  - ○ As managers: Expecting people to act outside of their personality causes breakdown of communication, leads to discontentment, misunderstandings, resentment, can reduce engagement and cost productivity. Add to that the personal stress of having to instruct, manage, correct, and ultimately discipline a person without understanding where they are coming from and suddenly, the idea of taking a few hours to learn how to understand your staff makes sense.
  - ○ Often, we try to force people into systems in which they do not fit. This causes problems while it creates monotonous cultures that limit the viability of your product. Take a look at the most interesting and successful business cultures today they welcome diversity and input.
  - ○ Many managers are thrust into their positions because they were ambitious technicians and very successful at their job. These managers need to constantly develop personality skills and emotional intelligence. They must be able to bring their staff into line with their vision.
  - ○ Lacking in the softer skills mentioned above often causes the new manager hours of stress because they don't have the needed reference points to efficiently connect with their staff.
  - ○ In personal relationships, understanding those you are to be most at ease with gives you the power to build bridges and come together.
- ➢ You know that people in all sorts of relationships are a huge investment of time and energy.

➤ You know that people need attention in every sort of relationship.
➤ It is counterproductive when companies or families get the best software and equipment, keeping it maintained with regular attention, but too often neglect the advancement of the people who use it.
➤ In families, we forget that children require a great deal of time and attention, that they learn from the adult. If the children in your home are taught to be unconscious, to neglect their own advancement, what sort of relationship are you creating with them?
➤ In your personal relationships, do you give attention to those you care about? How are you preemptively being smart and proactive in building great relationships?
➤ In your relationship with yourself do you give yourself time to feel loved and cared for? To have self-esteem arise from your attitude toward and treatment of yourself?
➤ As a leader, are you creating an environment where your people feel personally invested in the goals and success of your organization? A mission or vision statement on the wall is not enough to engage your staff. You need a company culture where they are willingly invested and engaged. A paycheck, while it matters, is not enough to get most people engaged.
➤ *Look at Maslow's Hierarchy: a paycheck is just survival stuff. It's needed and they won't come at all without it, but to get people invested there must be community and culture. To get them really excited the company has to be part of their advancement as a person. They must feel they have a purpose, and that they can work with purpose.*
➤ Any company based in western philosophy that is not thinking about the whole person they employ is falling behind the curve of having the best happiest and highest performing people.
➤ The majority will live for the money plus the culture and chances for purposeful growth and fulfillment.

- People engage nearly 40% more if you give them even a small amount of positive attention.
- Consider that production facilities hire maintenance staff to tune up and maintain their equipment. What are you giving the staff to grow and learn as people, how are you helping them get the newest technology and best out of their lives? If you look at the basic human needs (see Maslow's Hierarchy) you are reminded that stagnation keeps people from their potential and undermines the human drive for self-realization.
  - Mechanics have an array of highly technical and constantly updated equipment to protect your investment in your vehicle...
  - Yet, few companies invest in the advancement, maintenance, and tuning up of their people.
- *It is, in fact, your job as a leader and/or manager to find as many ways as you can to advance your people as humans, not just as workers. It doesn't have to be costly but in the big picture failure to do so will cost you a great deal.*
- **So, what have you done for your staff today?**
- Leaders, it is your job to hold your managers, and staff accountable for their performance, and it is your job to advance your performance. You can't advance your staff, your managers, or yourself if you don't bring in new information.
- When was the last time you gave your staff a new tool? Something that was nourishing to them personally, and to the betterment of the team.
- Entrepreneurs, want to get past that wall, find new creative flow, and get better results? Since you are the main engine that drives your business, have you looked in the mirror? Looked to see if you can do things differently? To consider what you might learn to be a better stronger, more aware business owner?
- Most people find they have some challenges with those they are closest to.

- When was the last time you sat down and thought about how the other person is feeling? It can be humbling to see your words and actions from another person's point of view. What if you had the courage to listen and see with their eyes and ears?
- How would it affect your patience if you did this?
- How would you be a better spouse, more loving partner, a better team member, if instead of inadvertently running the same old programs with them, you had self-compassion and spoke about your thoughts and feelings to them; giving them much-needed insight into your world?
- Think this is too much work? Talk to someone who has been fired or divorced. Ask them what it cost them to be out of a job or to split their assets, pay their lawyer, ask them how it feels to see their kids ½ the time.
- If we are more intelligent about relationships up front, much of the unnecessary suffering and struggle can be avoided.
- Some relationships need to end. But I do see relationships that become resilient, renewing the original positive, hopeful connection in a more mature way. This can be a professional or private relationship. Most profoundly, it can be your relationship with yourself. You can learn to see yourself, to build bridges by using this information, thus creating an extension of your positive, life-affirming relationship with yourself to others.
- Taking some time to bring better attention to the relationship isn't so hard to do. Some relationships don't work, that's ok. Many can improve; over the past 25 years, I have worked with leaders and managers to improve their teams and retain their experienced employees and with couples to see their old relationships in a renewed light. I have personally improved my self-esteem by learning to be more loving towards myself, this has helped me developed wonderful professional and personal relationships.

If we learn about ourselves and each other, consider each other as whole people in our interactions and apply wisdom in the way we treat people, we have better lives.

As a leader of a company, a team, a family or of yourself, think of the profound opportunity you have and the responsibility you carry.

You impact the quality of life of those around you!

Are they thriving?

Are they growing and advancing as employees and people?

Do they show up with enthusiasm?

Your responsibility is to impact and touch the lives of the people you serve, those who are helping you to reach your goals...have you brought them something new?

Given them the challenge and opportunity that will wake them up?

The time for the mundane grind of life is passed.

The time for new ideas, for a purpose, for compassion, for the renewal of humanity is here and now.

People demand it.

As a leader, you sought responsibility, it falls to your shoulders to provide tools that nourish and enrich those in the workplace.

You don't reach your goals without your people. The better off the people who work for you the easier the road to your goal.

9 Styles of the Enneagram

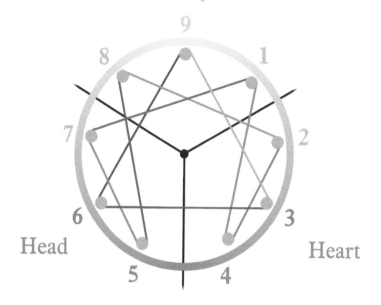

Perfectionist/ Reformer (1)

Helper/Giver (2)

Achiever/Performer (3)

Romantic/Individualist (4)

Intellectual/Investigator (5)

Loyal Skeptic (6)

Enthusiast/Epicure (7)

Challenger/Influencer (8)

Peacemaker/Mediator (9)

This information is learned in layers. Imagine that each new piece of information is like a set of old-school transparencies placed on top of what you learned previously. After reading this section you may have a good sense of your style. Still read through all the sections and learn about other styles.

Try to see it as a puzzle, bringing pieces of personality styles together. Use your imagination about how styles relate to each other. Look most deeply at yourself and those around you with curiosity. Leave behind defensiveness. If you judge others you will be judged, most definitely by yourself.

New ideas must be reintroduced, reinforced and seen from different angles to become part of the way our brain sees the world. You will do best as you approach this information with curiosity. Let it sink in over time. It is fun to notice new pieces of the system in action and learn.

Too often we are expected to know the answer before we have studied the subject. Therefore, I put the book in smaller sections, used bullet points, and included short narratives. My hope is to provide you the opportunity to go to a page or a section and in a few minutes use the information to build a picture of yourself and others. This empowers you to find connecting points, gives you insight into how the other person feels. It provides a chance to ask questions while you avoid taking things personally or making ill-founded assumptions.

You can quickly see from an overview of the 9 types on the following pages, that if you are Perfectionist/Reformer talking to a Loyal Skeptic, you are meeting in the need to get the details right, however the conversation might derail quickly if the Perfectionist is demanding loyalty to their vision before the Loyal Skeptic has faith in the vision.

Challenge your thinking processes to consider how these inherent differences and similarities are playing out. The Perfectionist might take the Loyal Skeptics' analysis as a positive, joining them in perfecting the project, or become offended if they take the questioning personally rather than as a normal part of the Loyal Skeptics' process.

Use the information in the following pages to get an overview of different people and ways they see the world; consider what they need, what they are trying to accomplish, and how they feel. Take note of what motivates individuals and how those motivations might align with or seem to challenge your own.

It is the ego's nature for many of us to push away from what we think is different. But emotional maturity requires us to see our ideas from broader points of view.

Think of the investment of your products and their long-range profitability by including diverse people in your creation and execution. You can sustain and plan for change in the products while you broaden your audience.

Note: We need each other, every single style brings winning qualities to a family and team.

When we can learn to see different points of view as assets, we are developing wisdom. Wisdom and emotional maturity could be very useful to the world right now.

Golden Rule:

"Do unto others as you would have them do unto you".

> Would you like them to hear you?
> To respect your point of view?
> To help you succeed?
> To share your vision?

You have the power to bring the Golden Rule to all you do!

Enneagram Style Overviews

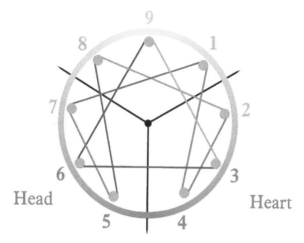

Perfectionist/ Reformer (1)

Helper/Giver (2)

Achiever/Performer (3)

Romantic/Individualist (4)

Intellectual/Investigator (5)

Loyal Skeptic (6)

Enthusiast/Epicure (7)

Challenger/Influencer (8)

Peacemaker/Mediator (9)

Perfectionist/Reformer (1):

> ➤ Sees the world in its perfected state, laments that others don't.
> ➤ Works to create or reform the world to match their perfect vision. Is willing to sacrifice much personal comfort to bring perfection and duty to life.
> ➤ Can cope with the world through humor, this is a winning strategy for them. One Perfectionist/Reformer I know copes with his trips to the sandwich shop at lunch by having an ongoing humorous narrative in his head. "It's like they are standing there picking their lunch meat and fixings for their sandwich for the first friggin time ever! Is this really their first time here?! Do they really not know that they can have ham or turkey, some yellow cheese like substance or some white one!?! Why are people so stupid?".
> ➤ Usually has very neat, crisp appearance even when casual. All the Perfectionist/Reformers I know workout because it is the right thing to do.
> ➤ These people are amazing at getting things done if they believe it is the right thing to do. While they can be casual, they are always clean, even when working at a job that requires physically strenuous labor, they hold themselves in a precision that inspires or intimidates. They will be the first in the shower to get fresh and won't relax until they are clean.
> ➤ Feels they will find fulfillment in the perfection of the world, looking to get it right so that they are closer to the Creator.
> ➤ One might assume that the Creator is perfection and therefore they would find their salvation in the success of the ideal work.
> ➤ Leads others best when they have learned to temper their demands with compassion.

Helper/Giver (2):

- Focuses on feeling/heart connections. These people long to connect, to know that they are valued because they are loving and help make the world a better place.
- Works to make others feel happy.
- Cheerleaders, they rally people together.
- Helper/Givers cope with the sandwich shop scenario through empathizing with what the counter help is going through or the point of view of others in line. Occasionally, they might side with the "poor" indecisive person but would likely see them as the one hurting the others. For example: "that poor kid helping people who can't make up their minds. How hard can it be to pick a meatball or decide if you want them to heat up your sandwich? I wish people paid more attention to how they treat each other and then they might not hold up this whole line. We all just want some food."
- They likely have an appealing appearance that invites connection. I have witnessed Helper/Givers make sure that they have a trustworthy appearance; have heard nurses say, "I want to wear scrubs that cheer up the patients. They are going through enough, if I can help them laugh, I am going to wear balloons on my top"! In the business world, these are the people who wear expressions of warmth. Princess Diana was a picture-perfect Helper/Giver. We all feel like we want to be in the comfort of their radiance. If they are not well cared for it is because they are overdoing for others.
- Often found in helping fields doing for others and being too busy to help themselves.
- Will never let a friend down.
- Can be a very successful leader, especially when they use their gifts to share and motivate their people towards a common goal/vision.

Achiever/Performer (3):

- ➢ Getting the job done is what matters to the Achiever/Performer.
- ➢ They most often have an upscale professional appearance. Appearance is part of the package. It's how they get things done, how to let people know that they mean business. These are folks who are likely to wear pressed perfect casual clothing.
- ➢ While most of us would like to have household help, Achievers are likely to get this help asap; because they have important things to do. They need others to help them with mundane, unimportant tasks so their attention is on big things with maximum return. No chit chat, things to do!
- ➢ You are most likely to have the Achiever/Performer offer "you fly, I buy!" They don't like the idea of waiting on things. If they are in line at the sandwich shop, they are too busy on their phone to notice how slow the line is, or they have ordered lunch through the app (online) and are just picking it up."
- ➢ Can be pushy about getting things done and forgetting others.
- ➢ Super-efficient, not always detail oriented.
- ➢ Rarely initiate personal growth unless they see a direct correlation to how it will make them better at getting things done, improve their image, or help them get what they want.
- ➢ Frequently found in sales and jobs with high visibility, or in management roles. If they are more introverted they will still be in demanding action-oriented roles, but less visible.
- ➢ They will make unilateral decisions or see external input as a waste of time. Unless they are very social, then they welcome outside input, but will most likely want to heavily influence the final decision and oversee it without having to get hands dirty.
- ➢ When the Achiever/Performer makes an intentional decision to care about others their hearts open and they become amazing mentors.
- ➢ They are motivated to do things to prove their value.

Individualist/Romantic (4):

- Feeling deeply, this person can have the emotional resilience of a superhero, or crumble hopelessly under the weight of their emotional burden.

- As professionals in the coaching or counseling field, no one stands in the storm of emotion more fearlessly with you. In their personal life, the amount of emotion they feel can be consuming. When balanced, the Individualist/Romantic can be an unwavering ally and a creative force, bringing their considerable emotional intelligence to manifestation through projects and collaborations. Be cautious of telling them how they should feel or what their art should look like.

- Having an appearance that is not average is key. Even if the Romantic/Individualist has a casual look, they carry it in a self-conscious nonchalance that shows them as the artist they are. I recently had coffee with a Romantic/Individualist friend. She wore greyish neutrals and is letting the grey come through into her blonde. She looked fascinating! I don't even think of grey as a real color, but I was in admiration of her style. I proceeded to notice that the set of her eyes and jawline mirrored the timeless beauty of Cybil Shepard. She responded with a mild polite smile, knowing that I meant well, but not amused at being "like" anyone else.

- The Romantic/Individualist at the sandwich shop is the person who is trying to make a sandwich unlike any sandwich ever made before. They have no interest in a sandwich numbered or pre-made…nope, that is too pedestrian. I want a meatball and olive sandwich, on that new bread, with the exact right veggies, and please don't over or under toast it.

- Through their emotion, their uniqueness, they find their own version, their own very personal connection with their reason for existing.

Intellectual/Investigator (5):

> Retreats into Information.
> They are deep inside their mind where they are seeking answers because the world doesn't give them comfort.
> While there is often an air of introversion, Intellectual/Investigators can be extroverted too. Remember that intro/extroversion relates to where we get recharged, the Intellectual/Investigator often reports feeling overwhelmed and drained by the presence of most other people. Even the most social of Intellectual/Investigators can appear to be retreating from the group.
> Information provides the Intellectual/Investigator with the stimulation that makes them feel alive. Social Intellectual/Investigators study in groups or talk about ideas, rarely talking about themselves.
> Information, ideas, or research that challenge the mind are nourishing to these people. They can be voracious consumers of data. Their challenge is to make it useful; to find ways to turn the knowledge into wisdom, through actions.
> Relies on knowledge and humor to relate.
> The Intellectual/Investigator can have surprisingly sophisticated tastes or be extremely practical and non-fussy.
> These people can be surprisingly absent-minded or exacting in their appearance but are not likely flamboyant.
> At the sandwich shop, they would likely order something simple, not wanting a fuss. There is a desire in the Intellectual/Investigator to not want to need much in the world.
> The Intellectual/Investigator, if stressed or in a state of anger. can push people away by intentionally not grooming or washing. It is a signal that they don't want you in their space.

Loyal Skeptic (6):

> Analytically Minded, the Loyal Skeptic weighs everything all the time. They usually feel driven to do what is right, to be a good person, and struggle to make the "best" most intelligent choices. Often seeing things in black and white, they can get lost or stressed out by shades of grey in the world, and feel all grey is ultimately black.

> Egalitarians with whom loyalty is earned, rarely given. To earn their faith, it must strike a chord in their heart and once that cord is struck their faith is immovable. They may have faith or dedications even to people or things that are not actually good for them; but once faith is given you will not move them.

> At the sandwich shop, this person is either going to order off the menu with no variations or be timid yet demanding about their analysis of ingredients. If they don't have faith in their order, may your soul be blessed, this is going to take a while (eyeroll that may lead to concussion).

> Loyal Skeptics can have a very hard push back against rules. They are Loyal, once they have determined through intense analysis what they chose to be loyal to, but they are not conformist. Unless they have decided to have faith in you, in which case they can become blindly conforming.

> With a staunch sense of equality for all people, including themselves, the Loyal Skeptic won't be told what to do, they will decide for themselves!

> In my experience they will make a point of their rights to self-determine: for example, they will wear shorts and sandals to the formal wedding, because "who are they to tell me what to wear!?

> Once they have figured out where their loyalty lies, they feel the relief of no longer having to analyze.

65

Enthusiast/Epicure (7):

➢ These folks would rather lead the show or party and let someone else make sure all their details are organized. They do however thrive when they pay attention to the details. This helps them get their big ideas on the ground.

➢ Enjoying life keeps them engaged until they become overwhelmed by the sheer volume of contacts on their phone.

➢ They have no qualms about deserving the best, most interesting thing they can have.

➢ They will quietly hope for something new or add a dash of something exotic. "yes, I'd love to add curry to my ham sandwich, please and thank you!" Next time, they will try that new mustard or other sauce. They are not going to labor over it at lunchtime though because they have other things to get on to. However, on a social outing, this is the pied piper leading you to the newest clubs, the freshest bands and looking for the thing you've never seen before.

➢ Usually, the Enthusiast/Epicure will put effort into their look. Sometimes to the extreme. In a business situation, they may conform in clothes but may not. If you find people having a great time pushing the fashion edge, you may have met an Enthusiast/Epicure! Even in a conservative setting, you will notice the person pushing the boundaries of fashion with a brighter colored shirt or wearing some piece the delights them.

➢ These people can often look for ways to make the world a better place, big humanitarian ideas, or kind-heartedness is part of their appeal. They are very averse to suffering and want to avoid it by strategizing to make life better, happier.

➢ They can struggle with coping with the day to day reality that life is demanding and often not glamorous. The Enthusiast/Epicure benefits from self-awareness and periods of rest without having others to overstimulate them.

Challenger/Influencer (8):

> These people see themselves in the role of leader and will usually take on the role if there is any sort of leadership void.

> As leaders, they look to see who is on their team and who is not. Never one to shy away from a good chance to prevail or expand their circle of influence you will find them defining and defending their borders.

> If you are "on their team" you are worthy of their loyalty and protection. This powerful person can be an amazing ally and a terrifying enemy. They are protective of their people and having significant energy will do all they can to make sure those they care for are well tended.

> In a healthy state, you will find them to be compassionate level-headed leaders that genuinely tend to the best interest of all concerned.

> They can move mountains, but in an unbalanced state, you have a heck of a bully.

> When left without direction or allowed to become bored Challengers can fabricate reasons for a fight, they need intensity and purpose into which they direct their energy.

> These folks tend to have an intense appetite, and some, find it hard to stay in healthy proportion. They may order too much or talk louder than others.

> At the sandwich place, this is a person likely to mention to the manager that they need more lunchtime counter help or to buy the guy behind them in line their sandwich. Most have a sense of grandness that can show up as generosity, boldly shared helpful opinions, or as unhealthy puffery.

> Challenger/Influencers can be found in many fashion fronts, power clothing is a real tool in this world. Not usually a beige fan, you are more likely to find power colors, fabrics that express an influential, substantial image.

Peacemaker/Meditator (9):

- ➤ Seeks to create a calm, safe world for all, because this is how they think they will find peace.
- ➤ To find peace, they must become self-aware and work to acknowledge and care for their feelings and thoughts.
- ➤ Peacemaker/Mediators find peace when they treat themselves as whole people and no longer allow themselves the illusion that evaporating their needs and feelings is pleasing to those they love.
- ➤ Often, they find themselves in conflict because of who they really are and who they want to be might uncalm the waters. These people are forces whether they admit it or not. The sooner they know they are powerhouses and become self-aware, the sooner they speak up and say: "I am going into my sweet cave, it's what I need, and I will see you on Monday", the sooner they embrace self-determination, the sooner they become happy.
- ➤ Peacemakers in their small state, where they are trying not to be a problem will order as simply as possible: "Yes, tuna salad on white bread." Ok, I will have that as a meal. Whatever is easiest! Those who have embraced their power are likely to find great pleasure in their food and drink.
- ➤ "What is wrong with yoga pants under a jersey? This is comfy." While a Peacemaker/Mediator will comply with the standard, my experience of them is mostly that they would be happy in something unfussy. If it is appropriate to their task or position, they will wear the power suit with the best of the rest of the players, but go home to comfy, unwind to something yummy, and be very willing to turn off the phone while they read or binge watch and pretend the world out there isn't a real thing.

The highest forms of understanding we can achieve are laughter and human compassion. – Richard P Feynman

Be Mindful of Our Common Humanity

If you use the awareness in these pages to be smarter about how you interact with others: you will ease your way in the world, regain lost energy, improve relationships, and enjoy more humor and grace.

Sometimes simply having the information about our differences and similarities gives us space to not take things personally. To allow each person to be different and perhaps enjoy those differences.

The human mind can be strangely literal about our own feelings/thoughts vs those of other people. We often think of ourselves as right and others as wrong or of others as superior and subjugate ourselves. This imbalance can be caused by many things. But if we see all humans as valuable, with things they are responsible to contribute, then we are more able to compassionately hear and speak our needs, wants, emotions and to contribute more readily to the whole.

We may not be the team leader, but we are on the team, and we count. This is purpose! We all have, need, and want to live with and for a purpose! Feeling alive in that gives us joy, juice for life! Support yourself and others in their purpose, or at least in doing things in a purposeful way.

We all house a lifetime of memories and experiences, cultural training that created our personality and world view. These are driving everybody's responses and behaviors at any given moment. Interpreting another person's lifetime of history against your own is impossible, and it is not what I suggest.

What I suggest is that as we learn to take responsibility for our own personality. At the same time, we can understand that people of another style have their own experience and that we accept that we are in this life together. Accept that we have to find a way to connect if we work together and have to find a way to accept the differences to thrive.

An example: As a powerful person, I really like Simon Cowell from the talent shows. He is clear, compassionate, to the point and doesn't want to waste time. He embraces fame and is unapologetic about the way he holds power. He has given thousands of people chances to showcase their talents, created employment and given us so much good stuff to watch! Remember when he was so grumbled about: people saying he is mean, too blunt, too direct, what gives him the right?

He has the right because he does. No one is compelled to go in front of him, but he owns power and uses it for the betterment of people. His results speak for themselves and if you watch the show, he clearly has a huge tender heart.

When we believe our own reactions and don't look deeper, we only see what is obvious through own filters, or we misinterpret the other person because we are reacting to them or fearful. Don't get me wrong, there are bad mean people in the world, but the first thing you need to do is take responsibility for yourself, your interpretations and emotions. Until you do this, you can't really tell much about others.

The man in my story who could only see an angry woman Challenger denied both of us the chance to heal something, his fear of strong female emotions, and my feelings about being too much. He ignored the tenderness, sweetness, and hurt because he did not like bold women. He did not see me, he saw my suffering, he did not see his fear of me, he projected onto me that I was the problem. And I paid him for the weekend! But I did use the information for self-awareness and growth, without that decision on my part, this book would not be happening, or a least not in the same way.

Step back and look at human interaction; you can see too much of the above dynamic happens. To learn to see things differently we must exchange our defensiveness for curiosity, to gain mental, spiritual, emotional strength by expanding our process. When we make a commitment to see ourselves and others as whole people, we can be less reactive, take things less personally. Reduce reactivity and create cooperation.

When we are building bridges to have better relationships with others, the destructive power of defensiveness becomes obvious. Too many shields and not enough awareness of what is truly a threat. Defensiveness destroys connection because it limits our vision and point of view.

Defensiveness also assumes that the other person is attacking us. What if they are simply sharing their opinion? Why should we shut each other down? What are we so afraid of that we can't tolerate another point of view? This pulls us into survival mode. We act as if people are their ideas. Ideas change! There is growth in allowing our thoughts to expand.

Looking at Maslow's Hierarchy of needs we see that for self-actualization: we must rise above our survival needs, embrace the tribe, find ourselves in the tribe with self-esteem. We all have the same basic needs and processes, we are simply influenced by our personality and cultures. We have many areas for growth and improvement as humans if you doubt that look at the news.

Accepting that we all must learn to put aside our defensiveness, makes it a little easier. I want to clarify here, that I am not discounting the need for a good defense. There are times when people are out to get you on a personal and international scale. But even if you are in a real survival situation, isn't it smart to be aware instead of reactive? To know you are defensive with consciousness rather than falling into old programs?

To gain emotional intelligence, and to have better relationships we have to stop and ask ourselves, how often are we only seeing others in the light of our fears and hurts? This means to be curious about and compassionate with each other (ourselves included). Know that we don't know most of what is going on for others and don't usually really take the time to understand our own fears and motivations. Too often we believe what we think with no further inquiry.

Curiosity and information give you the power to listen to people. If you hear that they are afraid of negative feedback or that they will be put off by what they call sugar coating; you can use those clues in your communication. Some folks need to hear the good first, they are afraid. They feel delicate and perhaps have some fear around power. Others need you to shoot from the hip but not at any vital organs. They will take feedback, but don't want to be your target.

Do you now overly accommodate them? NO! What you do is hear them, be curious about what must be going on inside of them, and where possible, adjust to being more effective in communication. Maybe you can remember to lead with a positive comment or to make suggestions for improvement in a gentler way. Sometimes try written instructions or feedback so they have time to process the information.

You have the power to eliminate the loss of time, productivity, and connection that comes from giving them information in a potentially non-productive way.

You can miss the mark if you are out of balance, this can be considered "too much" or unconsciously in the trance-like state of your style.

Knowing your type, you can observe when you are being "too much".

> Perfectionist/Reformers who are asking others to meet standards that are beyond excellence or a "job well done"; who feel a need to control every detail or stress out those around them are likely going too far.
> Helper/Givers who notice people avoiding them; or who find themselves oversharing (gossiping) about what is going on with others; or if you are trying to figure out how to get them to like you or manipulate a situation or person, you have probably gone too far.
> Achiever/Performers who have put themselves above others due to too much pride in their work; when you find yourself thinking "I

have to do more" or "people are all a bother, I wish they would just do what I want them to do", If you are dehumanizing people or pushing them to do more than they can or more than they feel is reasonable, you have gone too far.

➢ Romantic/Individualist who have lost themselves so much in emotion that they are not taking care of their daily life, or who are judging the profound hopelessness of human banality and pointlessness of life until they are paralyzed, have gone too far.

➢ Intellectual/Investigators who find themselves avoiding others to the point where you only have online friends, you only have work colleagues, or you find most of your conversations involve bitterness, sarcasm or the research of conspiracy, you likely have gone too far.

➢ Loyal Skeptics who don't have at least a few loving safe relationships, those who are blindly following anyone or anything without asking meaningful questions or who live in distrust of all life/the world, you are probably out of balance.

➢ Enthusiast/Epicures who are feeling confused or overwhelmed, lack a clear sense of how to proceed, have your phone blowing up faster than you answer it, feel overwhelmed by your own creation, you have gone too far in seeking to fill yourself up with the outside world.

➢ Challenger/Influencers who are often angry, feel the need to "tell it like it is" without considering other people. If you are hurting people's feelings often if you make people at work cry – you have gone too far and are creating enemies so you have battles to fight.

➢ Peacemaker/Mediators who feel like they are in a fog, working too much to manage their anger/rage, can't find peace in their day, are trying to please too many people, are probably lost in the stress of trying to make the world peaceful, instead of taking care of finding their own peace.

Knowing when you are too far into your own emotional challenges gives you clues about taking responsibility for your own state in communication (and in every area of your life!). In every communication, there are many sides. You are foremost responsible to bring your best possible self to the table, you are then responsible to do your best to be compassionate, curious, effective in your communication with another person. Evaluate as you go along, assuring that you stay present to the events as they occur.

We have a common language in our business cultures, along with cultural rules of engagement that help guide us. In personal relationships we have the same, "we don't swear in this house" or don't shout, but these agreements only go so far to making amazing, connecting, productive human interactions occur. Further, these rules can become warped with time. When the rules matter more than the people, they turn into part of the dehumanization problem.

Over time emotional communication has been excluded from normal life, and certainly from business communication. While emotion can get out of too personal, often cause drama, and are historically a rabbit hole. We have to find the language of emotional intelligence and balance our own trepidations. Leadership is not sufficient if we stop at making better widgets. If your goal is to make more widgets, then you are doing nothing more than creating and training robots. Human's create and produce. They are still the best form for getting things done that require interaction. To lead or manage human's is a great honor and challenge, no greater task can be put before you.

In your personal life, every relationship problem that has come to me, started by a person, not know that they were functioning poorly, communicating badly, or missing critical information on them self or the person they were attempting to join in a relationship.

Until we accept and embrace the differences of each other, we are going to struggle. When we make room for the whole human, you get better retention, more connection, better products, and more love.

76

Reflect on what happens when you isolate at least 1/3 of all your people who are primarily emotionally intelligent; worse, all people feel, so if you can't communicate feelings (within reason) you are shutting down all of your people to some degree. This is a huge issue because the emotions are present, they get repressed and then you have issues that run from passive-aggressive communication to resentment, to festering states that lead to sabotage or to people leaving the family, relationships, or blowing up in a meeting. This also leads to known stress-related health issues.

Over thinking kills the creative drive and leads to insomnia or exhaustion. Using too much of your physical power causes you to burn out, inappropriately use your body or collapse. The point is that we all have so much inside of us, and we are happier, healthier, live better lives when we are attentive to ourselves, and others as whole people. Whole meaning complex and not repressed in one area while overusing others.

For amazing communication in relationships, you need self-awareness on both sides, consideration of the other persons' motivations, the ability and desire to reach a decision, goal or share an experience, willingness to not agree, but work together. Enough presence to know that you are both having your own experience in your own world and meeting on a bridge to build together a shared world. The more awareness and personal responsibility you bring to the bridge, the better your mutual creation will be.

It is my intention in bringing this information to you, that you use it to uplift yourself. I ask that you "give yourself a break" and to extend this kindness to those around you.

- We all have needs and purpose that motivate us.
- We all have histories and filters on the world.
- All of us have hopes, dreams, people we care about.
- Every person you meet has the inner desire to be validated.
- We all have power in each other's lives.

You don't need to know all these details about others. If you treat them in a way that does not cause suffering, that may be the best you can do. Remembering their humanity reminds you of your own.

When you can connect through intentionally thinking about who they are, what they need, what drives them, you are making a powerful choice. You are deciding that this relationship is going to be successful, productive and compassionate.

- We are wired for compassion, but we also become wired for success, competition, and control, this happens through our fears, our past, and misunderstandings.
- Everyone puts up walls, defends their position, and carries around old hurts that shape their world view. This is a normal reaction to the stressors we face growing up and throughout our life.
- To advance in our purpose, our jobs, and as people, we must put an end to the suffering that each person carries around; at the very least, we can make a conscious effort to not cause more suffering.
- While we have the most control in our own world, we do have the power to affect one another. I have found that those people who don't feel they can affect others are the most stressed and controlling or hopeless and depressed.
- Having an effect does not mean getting them to see it our way, it means, learning enough about each other to find an agreement that you can both buy into. Sometimes, you will meet those who don't want to get to an agreement. But most people will meet you if you show them respect and make a genuine effort to understand them, show respect, and share yourself in the process.
- Suffering often comes from unmet needs. These may be actual or perceived. Many of life's experiences get stuck replaying in our subconscious mind, emotions, or thoughts.

All Humans Have Needs - Maslow's Hierarchy

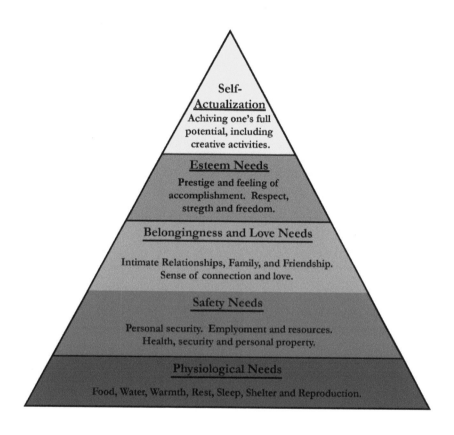

To lift ourselves up, our needs must be met.

Our workplace is tied to many of our needs. It is important that we feel safe at work, emotionally, mentally and physically.

Sometimes we ignore our mental or emotional states. When we do this, we send a subconscious message to ourselves that we are not safe, thus undermining our wellbeing, increasing stress, decreasing our ability to contribute and enjoy our work.

To mature as people, to self-actualize, we use tools that help us upwards along the pyramid of needs.

We can't segregate our self-esteem, from our state of mind, work life, or other parts of our life.

Self-esteem and state of mind are constants.

When we repress or hide our true feelings, needs, fears, desires, or lose our sense of purpose; survival mechanisms kick in reducing our feelings of wellbeing.

Compassion in the workplace means to treat ourselves and others as whole valid people; to empower ourselves, even when others don't see us. To realize our potential is based on our self-esteem, which is based in our self-compassion and self-awareness.

We are wired for compassion. We also become wired for success, competition, and control. These don't have to be at odds. In fact, if you look at communities where compassion is a core value, you see longevity and success. One of my clients comes to mind. As a Giver/Helper, she moved up the ranks in her company. She had high engagement, retention, and employee satisfaction. This was because she treated all her staff of over 150 people with compassion, dignity, and looked to help them advance.

Look at the loyalty given to public figures like Princess Diana, and Mother Theresa, see how people are drawn to and inspired by those who humanize others.

Employee evaluation polls tell us that if a manager shows care for the employee through positive personal feedback or through expressing confidence in them when the manager gives a new task, engagement from the employee improves by 39 percent.

39 percent is an impressive return on your most costly investment: your people. Therefore, among the most positively impactful things a manager

or leader can do, is to learn about the people in their charge. You would learn a product, or a software program, you equally must learn about your people.

In personal relationships, the people you love, don't share your world view, and what's more, they don't need to for a happy loving relationship to exist. How many families would struggle less if they stopped needing their kids or spouse to think like them? Remember back to your teen years. Think about how much better you feel when you find people who let you think your own thoughts and process your own way. People still need each other, need to share ideas, information and to share the worlds they created. But what if we met each other on the bridge, shared and allowed each other our own worlds. Sharing ideas to see how we messed up and considering the difference to see what we can learn from each other.

The Enneagram can help us to expand our sense of letting each other in, finding common ground, hearing different points of views without being threatened if we don't agree.

Everyone puts up walls, defends their position, and carries around old hurts. This is a normal reaction to the stressors we face growing up and throughout our life. To advance in our purpose, our jobs, and as people, we must put an end to the suffering that each person carries around, or at least make a conscious effort to not cause any more suffering.

Apply compassion in all your human interactions:

➤ If you feel negative emotions start with being aware of your own emotions and expand out to others. This means, if you are angry, ask why YOU are angry. It is rarely the other persons' fault that you are having an emotion.
➤ Occasionally you are dealing with someone who is not normally functional, and they will enjoy your pain. These are toxic people.

- Most often the pain is caused by something in your mind or emotion being triggered by the other person. The mind quickly goes to us vs them and makes the "other" the enemy. This is how dysfunction protects itself.
- Look at the other person, do you really see that they set out to harm you. Not to be naïve, because sometimes people intend harm. But this is not the norm.
- Step back and understand that you can take responsibility for the emotion without repressing it. You must do this, even if the other person is toxic and trying to upset or harm you.
- Notice it, understand it, take responsibility for what you do with the information that your emotions are giving you.
- Avoid clichés like I am going to take the high road. This is a way to gloss over or candy coat your feelings and to put the other person down while you aggrandize yourself.
- Be professional and respectful of yourself (and others) as a whole person. Emotions are information, either about your own feelings, the situation, maybe about how the other person is approaching you, or perhaps you are getting a gut feeling about the subject.

A few Components of Compassion include:

- Forgiveness: We must stop energizing the negatives from the past to progress as people.
- Our minds hold onto hurts to help protect us from repeating the same mistake or getting hurt again. To forgive is to see the past in its proper place; to see ourselves and others in the present moment and face the truth that making mistakes is part of being human.
- Communication: With ourselves, each other, our support system or our maker. Listen to the whole story, including the facts now. Most often you are safe. Most often if you had been honest in the moment you would not be holding onto the hurtful experience now. Clean up

what you can and avoid creating more suffering by using one of the many tools that are abundant in this book and in the world around you.

➤ Learn from communication and kindness; allow yourselves to accept feedback, ask others to receive your thoughts and feelings, with agreement give others feedback.

➤ Be accountable for mindful planning and non-personal analysis of data. This means we are not our mistakes, don't hide them, avoid them or hold on to them.

➤ Self-respect: Only you have the power to properly speak on your behalf because only you know how you feel and what you think.

➤ It is easy to see where someone's self-esteem is based on how they treat themselves. Do better!

➤ One of the most helpful components of compassion is to endeavor to understand.

➤ To understand each other is the basis to reclaim our natural disposition for compassion, communication, and having joy in community.

➤ When we understand, we can take responsibility for ourselves, can forgive ourselves and others more easily.

➤ Developing patience with our differences, using communication tools to become more productive, avoiding impasses and time/energy wasted on dysfunction or misunderstanding.

➤ We become more valuable to the team when we put in the effort to be compassionate.

➤ Suffering is on a continuum: it can be a nagging toothache, an emotional longing, or a health issue. It can be subtle, an emotion you deny, a lack of love, or need of affirmation of your worth as a person.

➤ We all suffer, it is part of the human condition, compassion is the only antidote.

Compassion is to feel with others. It is to wish to end all suffering.

This is a natural human state and a consciously chosen state of mind.

It is to recognize how another living being feels, to feel with them, to humanize them. To wish they did not hurt.

Most young children possess it, they will come and pat the hand or offer some form of comfort to a person suffering. But we are rather obsessed with happiness and pain avoidance. Which differs from compassion. We fear the emotions we don't know how to handle, those we judge as "bad". If we feel helpless to resolve our emotions, we can repress or become hardened toward them. This extends to others, we don't welcome them as full people, we want them to behave in a "less emotional" or less dramatic way. What is often happening is that one person doesn't know how to help the other person and they are trying to make it all go away.

This is partly because if parents don't know how to help children cope with their emotions, the children never develop the skills to look closely at themselves. This can be blatant, but also sneaky. Parents who allow themselves and their kids to zone out, who distract rather than deal with the emotion, are teaching repressing. Don't mistake me, have fun, go to amusement parks, entertain yourself, but not to cover up or hide from our very human emotions.

In watching body language, I have noticed that people react to others who are in an emotional state the same way they act towards those with colds. Some of us lean in and want to help, others literally, physically draw away.

> Side note: we do affect each other. This is where the idea that we are a mirror for each other is used. People can bring each other down, this is especially true if you are identifying with their emotional reaction instead of seeing it as a passing state. Emotions are messages, some messages are clear, others need to be worked out, just like thoughts.

> If you fear another person's emotional state, unless they are being violent, you can be sure that you fear your own inner state. This is a moment when you must bring in presence: what is really happening now? Am I threatened? What is the message in the emotion? What is threatened by the emotion? Is this triggering my repressed emotion or challenging an idea that you hold as part of your identity. The emotions are a body of intelligence, just like the mind. Sometimes things need to be worked through to get to a whole answer. Ideas are not always clear, but we have normalized working them out. Be respectful of emotions and you will have a much happier life, along with better results on your team, in your home, and in every sort of relationship.

> If someone has a chronic issue, you might not have the skills to help them resolve it, that is not really your job. Your place is to be kind and if you see a chronic issue or a prolonged difficulty for people, then suggest they seek professional help.
>
> Occasionally, people are enjoying the drama. But most people, most of the time, are not enjoying painful emotions. In many situations simply offering a bit of human kindness is enough. At least do not treat an emotional person like they are repulsive.

The human emotional condition is developed when we are young. It is a tough experience for most of us. If it is handled with kindness and compassion, we have more resilience. I am not saying to indulge the emotion either. You can't create a life run by emotion. It's an important balance to see and feel an emotion, understand it, but not let it own you. Few are masters of this, but the practice of it is crucial. Check my video channel to learn more about this practice.

You don't need to fear "catching" each other's suffering or emotional state. If you are conscious and stay in the present, you can relate, have compassion, and let go of the other person's suffering. Trust that the healing process of the Universe will help them. Do what you can without getting lost in their process.

We are repressing or avoiding our own emotions, therefore when we care for others, their pain triggers and multiples ours. It is not our job to carry their burden but to offer comfort and support. Therefore, each of us must do as much of our own emotional healing as possible. We also benefit from our tribe's supportive compassion when we are hurting.

It is crucial to be self-aware with a mind towards taking responsibility for our emotions. This is presence. We can help without becoming the other person or absorbing their pain, as we can accept help and retain our dignity, becoming vulnerable to a part of what makes us whole.

Think about wholeness. Body, Mind, Spirit, Emotions, Culture, Family, Epigenetics, Personality. These are all part of each person's life. Without wholeness, we won't ascend on the ladder of needs to self-actualization.

We crave purpose for a reason, it is what drives us forward as humans. Without all your parts in place, it's like driving a car without a transmission or having the best power train, but no wheels, things won't function without all the parts being attended to.

We suffer when we don't answer the call of compassion, we miss the depth of feeling, the lessons to be learned and in our avoidance of pain, we don't learn to bear our own trouble with grace, but rather with compartmentalizing and repressing emotions that would be better expressed and healed.
We languish without compassion because we feel alone in the world when the truth is: we are all human together.

The essence of being human has an underlying wisdom that bonds us in a common experience, in universal reality. This makes us inseparable even as we build our own world pretending to be so very individual. We use this knowledge to give us the courage to build bridges to each other. People often don't see how much alike we all are. The mind moves towards protection, seeing the differences as roadblocks and harming our ability to connect.

Harm to others is learned through fear and abuse of power, it is learned behavior, coupled with our lower human instincts.

Often adults normalize punishment and blame. Don't get me wrong here: children need correction, guidance and sometimes punishment, they absolutely need to know that actions have consequence! What they also need from adults is to learn to think through their actions before punishment is needed.

Considering that the human brain doesn't mature until it is in its 20s, little humans do a poor job sorting out what to keep or what to not repeat from the adults they grew up around.

Therefore, we see a great number of bad habits passed from one generation to the next. This is why I am referring to our childhoods in this book that is for adults, leaders, managers, parents, friends, partners etc. Because most of what is messing with your team, your family, your love life, starts when people are children. It's just like math, the numbers you have been giving in the equation will determine how you solve the problem.

To get to the goal, solution, or outcome you want, you must know the numbers you are using to get there. If you try to blindly tell everyone the answer, you are taking unnecessary risk.

If you are bold and brave enough to look at the places most others avoid, you will automatically improve your odds of success, and increase your ease on the road to your goals. Relationships are the foundation of most things, these are formed by people, people are formed by their past, their choices, their personality, their culture, and how they treated each other/are treated.

Your choice is to build bridges, not to change them, but to create amazing compassionate relationships that will improve your success, your health, and quality of life in every area.

If a parent focuses on blaming and teaching through post-event punishment, the child will grow up pointing their fingers at others. This teaches the child to feel bad about mistakes, it's like animal training but does not create an environment for learning to think up front or help them learn to think about how to make better choices. We carry this esteem killing behavior into the rest of our lives.

Children blame, avoid, and lie because adults do. People do these things because they are afraid of getting punished, or of having their safety threatened by being caught.

Children protect themselves by compartmentalizing or justifying their actions because adults around them model this behavior, they also fear being wrong. It is an outcome of fear, blame, and punishment vs forethought. Forethought is awareness of yourself, your motivation, the potential outcome, and doing your best to make a good choice.

I make these points so that you can become aware of the ways you learned to operate in an unconscious manner. Everyone does the above. We learn and teach what we have learned. If we choose to see the dysfunctional behavior we are currently using and apply the things we are learning we can become smarter, more forgiving, compassionate people. We can operate with forethought. We can make much better choices if we learn about what we have hidden from ourselves and intentionally see it.

The human brain will take the "path of least energy use". This is a primitive function that helps us to conserve energy in survival situations. It's similar to how easy it is to sit and not move vs going to work out. Our system needs to flex, exercise, stretch, be mentally stimulated, emotionally enriched and challenged. Yet, we all have this survival program in us to conserve energy. So, we have an explanation about why it's so hard to think preemptively about things, but do we want to let it be an excuse that keeps us in survival mode?

Are you going to settle with normalized narrowmindedness, allowing yourself to choose the path of least resistance and develop lazy brains and bodies? Or are you going to put effort into being conscious?

It is a tradition for one generation to gripe about the next. The younger people are always accused of being lazy, wrong, not respectful, but who taught them. The unconsciousness travels through training and osmosis from one generation to the next. It is only through an awakening and lots of connections to new ideas that we find our way towards a better tribe. The problem we face with blame and punishment vs forethought is the former keeps pulling us into survival mode (the good old days), while the latter pulls us up toward self-actualization, which I believe means connection and clear communication with our Creator.

The apparent chaos of moving towards self-actualization scares most people and we retreat into the comfort of survival behavior. But we need to challenge ourselves, to find the courage to face our fears. If we allow ourselves to remain in this mental/emotional laziness, the constant hate, wars, and suffering created by people entrenched in survival mode will continue to dominate the human experience.

We each must work towards improving the human condition. If you are a person of faith, you know the paradox of caring for the sick vs teaching them to fish. This is difficult to reconcile, we can't really tell what the other person's burden is because we aren't aware of or we are obsessed with our own. It's tricky to know how to help and we must consider boundaries, working to know where the line is between helping others, hurting ourselves and creating dependency.

No one should be dependent on another more than they are reliant on themselves and the Creator, yet no person should be alone and uncared for per the teachings we hold dear – the inner knowledge of the laws of human decency. This is why we avert our eyes when we see the desuetude and feel shame or anger because we don't feel that we have the knowledge or the means to help them.

The best we can do is listen to our inner voice, our spirit or soul, and do our best in each moment to listen for what is wiser than our human mind to guide us. The human mind can't sort out everything we are faced with, but it can learn to listen to wisdom. It learns when you intentionally see yourself and others as whole people and choose compassion.

Compassion has been called the foundation for real intelligence and is the path to wisdom.

We tend to avoid compassion in the workplace and too often in our life. We fear that our ideas about ourselves and that our worlds will be shaken to the core if we have to feel what others are feeling. We must take responsibility for how we affect each other. It might mean we have to alter our behavior and to deal with the fact we have not been good to others. Almost no one is being the best human being possible. So that we can see the hard things about ourselves, we have to start out with forgiving ourselves for the judgments we place on our humanness. From here we reclaim our true sustainable power to make choices that are of benefit to the whole and the individual in many ways.

Compassion starts with ourselves. We can't grow and build bridges if we are being hard on ourselves.

We collectively have come to this point in our individualizing that puts us at odds with those who see things differently. The idea that: if you don't stand for something, you will fall for anything, has attached itself to our egos, rather than to qualities build character and make us better people. So often it has made us hard towards each other and increased our pain.

Many have replaced the purpose of their lives with making money or achieving a goal. There is nothing wrong with money, it is a tool and it is wonderful to have.

Money represents our ability to take care of our survival needs. There is an imagination that money is scarce, which pushes people into survival mode, and people will do dehumanizing things to assure their own survival. This is the danger of some of our behaviors today.

We are pushing fear in the media and people are stimulated to believe their survival is threatened. Think about this, what could drive one person to hurt another: usually it is feeling threatened by the other. If we see the truth, we are not usually a threat to each other's survival.

To be clear competition is fun. It keeps us honing our skills, advancing and improving. It's just that we are not usually competing for our survival. Some people are, that is a different story, and a horrible shame considering that we have enough for everyone's basic needs to be met.

Money is never the goal of human life. It is a tool. It is nice to have more money than you need, but you can't let the survival mechanism push you to harm others in the pursuit of money.

It is not the Creator, you can't take it with you, and if you hurt others to acquire money you are damaging yourself. You are allowing your base fear to control you.

Same with power or fame, read the above.

Ignoring others' suffering is quite painful. The suffering is there whether we are looking at it, it is in the commonly held reality. We are affected by the suffering of our fellow humans.

We do have to take care of ourselves, but if we ignore the chances life gives us to improve the lives of others, we are failing at the most basic sense of decency. You don't have to give all your money away or hire an incompetent to be compassionate. You can be thoughtful of those around you and give them as much grace as you would like to receive. Further, you can bring compassion by doing even small things for larger causes that improve the human condition. It may not be your job to feed the homeless directly, you have the power to help those who do.

At home, you can hear your kids out, and realize that them having their own point of view, is not actually a threat to you. If you listen, learn and share, you will in most cases end up with a more joyful relationship. In the end, if they are going to disagree with you, they will. If you destroy parts of who they really are by pounding them into your image, you will have a miserable person or horrible break with them.

Hiding out versus seeing the truth

We all hide out emotionally sometimes.

It is simply a thing we do and can get away with because it is a learned behavior.

Like it or not Santa Claus is a collective lie that we agree to tell. If you don't agree to tell the Santa Claus lie you are in big trouble.

Kids are brought up to believe this, then....it is gone. The adults telling them not to lie just told them a heartbreaking lied. It's confusing to the child and sets the child up to suffer a great loss of faith in the parent and in goodness. Still, we defend this lie with vigor because we want life to be good, to be happy, we long to believe in generosity and miracles.

We fear seeing that, in fact, we are Santa. If we face the goodness in us, then we are called to live in a better way.

We are the bringers of goodness, hope, generosity, kind deeds without seeking reparations, we are what is good in the world. There is a part of us that longs to bring joy to each other. I believe this is the part of us most connected to the Creator because I believe the Creator wants joy for all.

We hide our power like we pretend we are not Santa Clause. Maybe because if we see all the good in us, we might also have to see the challenges. I promise you can handle everything inside of you. Not looking at ourselves is hiding from our privilege, our greatness, and the things we have the responsibility to change.

Santa Claus is a collective fantasy of what we could become to each other.

Every culture has these lies that we agree to. We hide out. We don't tell people how we are really feeling. It's one thing if we don't want to hurt their feelings, it's another if we just don't want to be vulnerable with ourselves or each other.

95

- But what are we hiding from ourselves?
- What lies do we let ourselves believe?
- Which ones do we hold on to, because we need to keep ourselves safe from the shadows we don't know how to cope with?

To be self-reflective, look at the information about your style and learn about yourself. You will find out that you are more wonderful than flawed and that what you thought are flaws are more about you getting stuck in survival mode. There are tools to calming survival and moving toward thriving.

Fearing the revelation of our flaws is so silly, we can all see each other's flaws, which is the point of the teaching that says to take the plank out of your own eye instead of trying to take the splinter out of another person's!

We see others faults and hide from ourselves. Look at the self-esteem issues that arise for people. How many of us wish we realized how attractive we really were in high school instead of living in anxiety about our looks?

If you run a company, you want to know where your weaknesses are. When you own a home or a car you do maintenance, why: because you want it to be functional and there are multiple systems that must work together for success.

Knowing your own strengths, motivation, weaknesses, challenges, and triggers gives you real power in the world because it means you are making conscious, more effective choices.

- Do you need to tell the truth (to yourself) more?
- Are you hiding out, not leaning in, avoiding tough feelings?
- Are you letting fear stop you from enjoying and doing your best job?
- Are you making sure that your needs are being met?
- Are you living with self-respect? Self-compassion?

➤ Is there a way you can use your knowledge of yourself and others to build a bridge?

you can see, asking questions in self-reflection is very important if you are advance your understanding, your compassion, your self-awareness.

➤ This can be quick, fun and interesting, treat your inner workings as a puzzle or a mission of discovery. This is needed to become conscious about things you've been hiding from yourself or others.

➤ Use a journal, a counselor, a friend, contemplate, find out what's really going on in there!

Use this information to build bridges

> ➢ Read through the Enneagram information.
> ➢ Consider the things you learned about how others see and experience the world.
> ➢ Consider at least 3 ways that you can connect with or relate to another type of person.
> ➢ Think about 3 ways that you are different from another person.
> ➢ Use the charts to consider your different needs, motivations, and passions.
> ➢ Find an agreement with a person. There is always at least one yes! Find it and build from there.
> ➢ Don't start by taking corners to prove your point.
> ➢ Remember your responsibility is to get the job done right and well. Too often sibling rivalries or creating fiefdoms rob work of its joy and productivity.
> ➢ Increase your respect for another person's point of view. No one is an island, you need them.
> ➢ Think about ways you could benefit from hearing another's point of view.
> ➢ Consider the way you would like to experience your relationship. Think in terms of "how can I personally understand my spouse, child, friend or family members?"
> ➢ Be curious about what is going on in their thoughts and feelings.

Qualities worth your attention:

- Compassion, Mindfulness, Presence: These are very popular words these days, but they have been the steadfast and successful teachings for as long as we have recorded history.
  - The most basic understanding of these brings us to a foundation for interaction with life. Our relationship to these words and concepts tells us about our relationship to ourselves, people and the whole world.
- Compassion = The recognition of what makes all people suffer, and the desire to end that suffering.
- Mindfulness = Paying attention to our thoughts and putting them in the proper place, giving our minds attention to a subject or action without distraction. Redirecting our thoughts gently and consistently as to not create mental whiplash as we train ourselves to focus. This simple action reduces errors, increases our ability for emotional/mental resilience, and gives us a great deal of energy. It also enriches everything we do.
- Presence = You are a whole person, it is compassionate to treat yourself and everyone else as such. It is recognizing things, feelings, thoughts from the past for what they are, freeing yourself to enjoy the present moment with greater comprehension and satisfaction.

.

Parts of Personality

There are many in-depth works about the following information and the Enneagram. Most of them are very good and I hope that they increase in usefulness to you after you have grasped and are applying the basics in this book.

In working with companies and families, I have found about 1 in 20 will call to have an assessment and work with me, but about 1 in 35 will go and buy other books and study the subject further. Meaning for most of you this will be the extent of the information you have on the subject.

For this reason, I want you to be able to leave here with a comfortable working understanding that becomes a useful part of your home or business culture.

My experience has been that I tend to get frustrated and not enjoy learning as well if I am missing some of the building blocks of a subject. Having a foundation, a mutual understanding of word meanings, and the basic ability to make sense of the subject is important.

Most likely you are more intuitive and emotionally intelligent than you realize. My hope and goal in this book are to wake up some of the amazing compassion and emotional intelligence inside of you. To support you in utilizing your hidden intelligence.

For me, too often I assume I know the meaning of a word that I don't use often and then end up having to rethink it in the context of the subject. I am attempting to save you time. Most of us learn better when we aren't guessing at pieces of information.

Since there is a lot of popular psychology out there and terms are sometimes used in different ways, I am hoping to be extra clear with this book and especially in the following explanations. See the following pages for more insight on these areas of personality influence.

Introvert/Extrovert (ambivert)

➤ Intro/Extrovert – where we charge our batteries
➤ Instinct – how we relate to others to survive
  ○ Social,
  ○ 1:1,
  ○ Self-Preservation
➤ Style (type) of Personality
➤ Head/Heart/Body – groups of styles with similar qualities.
  ○ Thinkers/Feelers/Gut responses in the Enneagram this is also sometimes referred to as:
  ○ Thinkers: thought oriented/fear based/anxiety prone
  ○ Feelers: feelings oriented/emotional
  ○ Body: Feels things in the gut/body, anger-prone
➤ Wing(s) – what's on each side of your main style
  ○ These styles influence us and can reveal additional clues about the way we behave in the world.
➤ Arrow(s) – resources and signs of stress.
  ○ These are connection points that can help us or reveal that we are functioning in stress.
➤ Subtypes – influences from family, culture, education, personal development. As you can imagine this is a very in-depth topic. For our purposes know that if you feel that you have a strong subtype, you do. Like a secondary identity that feels very close to home even though you know your main style is where you land when you strip it down to your most basic motivation.
➤ Self-forgetting – forgetting yourself in favor of caring for others, a way to avoid yourself is to pile yourself with other people's thoughts and needs.
➤ Self-aggrandizing – sees self as the center of things, most important or tries to inflate importance, sometimes at the expense of others.

Knowing about yourself and others' fundamental natures helps to avoid feeling personally hurt when different motivations and needs are driving people around you.

We all tend toward our own view of the world, but for productive, successful relationships we must see things through their eyes,

> ➤ When you are aware of the different needs that people have, you can consider how to meet your own needs; and how to accept others as they are, thus you can accommodate or at least be compassionate while remaining personally genuine.
> ➤ While the instincts are about how you relate to others in survival, it is not the same as Extrovert/Introvert.
> ➤ Extrovert means you gain energy from going outside of yourself.
> ➤ Introvert means you gain energy from going inside yourself.
> ➤ Ambivert means you are equally balanced between the two as a means of charging your proverbial batteries. Most of us are both introverts and extroverts, one is usually more clearly dominant. Think of it as a sliding scale, no one is happy always being alone, and everyone needs a break from the demands of the crowd.
> ➤ For example, I know a social introvert who has a very large circle of friends and is very outgoing, however, after almost exactly 2 hours, she retreats into her own world because her battery has been drained by socializing.
> ➤ Another friend is an extroverted 1:1. She leans into groups and projects "out there" connecting with lots of people, but her preference is to build deeper 1:1 relationship as soon as possible. The group is a great place to get lots of extrovert energy going, but she feels much happier in 1:1 conversation and experiences.

Instincts

Learning about the survival instincts through the Enneagram point of view has been a game changer for me and many of my clients. This piece of information has made it so much easier to be patient with other people's process. It has helped many managers to implement simple strategies to bring their team's together.

Summary: we are all driven to survive. We all have different ways we feel we will survive. While we all have all three instincts, one is more pronounced, the others fall into second and third place.

One of the biggest issues I see is that people of different survival instinct don't realize that everyone doesn't have the same ideas how to survive.

For example, a self-preservation survival instinct will hold themselves in a body language that is closed off until they feel safe, but a social person might take this as a rejection of their openness and need for connection. Many people get off on the wrong foot this way.

An extroverted social person can seem very intimidating to the self-preservation person. All that energy blowing up in the room and the expectation to meet it. Fear makes us arrogant, so when the two above meet they tend to get in their corners and make each other wrong.

Our world has traditionally celebrated the outgoing and bold, putting the quieter person in lesser esteem. The problem with that is that we miss the genius of the quiet person and dehumanize them. Also, the loudest person is not always the smartest, just the boldest.

The social person tends to like brainstorming on the spot, a self-preservation person, would need to know that a meeting is for brainstorming, and be given a set time for the experience.

Good meetings start with an agenda that recognizes the differences in people's needs for feeling safe. Feeling safe allows for better connection, more bridges and less miscommunication or the time draining drama of personal offenses.

In the case of the 1:1 person, I must warn you that Enneagram world doesn't seem to know what to call this style. I have seen the following descriptions: Sexual, 1:1, Charming Person, Intimate. I am sure there are more.

Here is an experience I had in a workshop led by a 1:1: We were in a Q&A after the mid-day session. The workshop leader was answering my question and I felt him so open with me, it felt very intimate and I felt very well attended to; when he moved onto the next person, I felt this pull, like, wait, "I thought we had a thing, and now you are being so intimate with her!" These people make you feel their presence with you, and when they focus on you, it feels very good. We all want attention after all!

All styles are needed in our life.

➤ We need to be in our tribe, to have safety in numbers.
➤ Sometimes being self-sufficient is the best safety measure.
➤ Making people feel their importance and yours creates a real connection.

We can, of course, develop skills to help us balance these. If you are very social but deplete yourself and don't pay enough attention to self-preservation things like your health or financial situation, that's an issue you can learn tools to correct.

If you are so involved in 1:1 relationship that you are lost in other people's lives, you need to reorganize and draw on the other instincts where it means getting more involved on a less personal level or see where you need more self-persevering.

Those with strong self-preserving instincts must intentionally see that they are not threatened. It is important to be more objective about their opening up to others, and intentionally building trust. Being cautious of projecting negativity onto other people to have an excuse to stay in their cave.

You will note that some of these qualities can be similar to the qualities you find in the personality styles.

Social

<u>We, All, Together</u>

- ➤ I walk into the room lit up to talk with the group. Energized by interaction!
- ➤ Let's do this!
- ➤ Groups are fun, exciting and great places to meet people.
- ➤ Gatherings are my playground.
- ➤ To get the best out of me, let me know I am part of the group, let me talk with others, brainstorm and give me clear priorities showing me how these are good for all of us!
- ➤ We are all safest when we are together.
- ➤ The more we know and understand each other the better for the team.

1:1

<u>Us, You & Me</u>

- ➤ 1:1s are also referred to as Intimate or Sexual instincts.
- ➤ I prefer 1:1 as a description in the workplace for obvious reasons.
- ➤ 1:1s like to connect with individuals or small groups.
- ➤ Don't take it personally if I am giving someone my undivided attention.
- ➤ Approach me and let me know you want to connect.
- ➤ Get most done in small teams.
- ➤ Feel safest when they have one or more 1:1 relationship they can count on.
- ➤ Prefer to brainstorm in smaller groups but can usually meet the demands of the social situation.

Self-preservation

Me, Then Us

- Social situations present dangerous variables.
- Excellent at seeing things that others miss.
- Prefer a clear set of expectations and an agenda over brainstorming.
- Large groups of people present too many variables to keep everyone safe.
- Treasure self-reliance and independence.
- Need time and reason to trust.
- Let SP types move towards you. It is not personal for them to hold back, it is part of a useful strategy of evaluating the situation before they jump into it.

Things to note:

1) All of these styles are in every person.
2) Your instinct is likely inherent in your being. You can see it in infants. It seems to be there or develop before our personalities.
3) Each personality style has all three instincts within each style. They stand on their own, yet they influence the person.
4) You can have social introverts and extroverted self-preservation people because they address different needs that a person is meeting.
5) Being sensitive to this can help us not take things personally;
   a. I tend to enjoy people who are deep thinkers, this will often connect me to introverts. But I am a social extrovert. This means that I have to be conscious that as I am getting started in public, they are just about ready to crash, feeling drained by the demands of being social. I watch them be sensitive to when they are fading. I used to take this personally. Thinking they were bored with me or didn't like hanging out. It was not at all personal to me, just what they needed to survive.

107

6) I used to get nervous when people connected then moved on. I didn't understand that they are just deep connectors, and it's not personal that they are now connecting with another person. Their natural way of relating can create jealousy, I am not sure they realize how they give others the humanizing attention that we all look for in the world. Many people long for intimacy, and they can feel uncomfortable with it. They drink it in and feel a bit left out when the 1:1s attention shifts to another person.

Healthy practices such as boundaries and not taking other people's behavior personally help us to cope, but observing and understanding make good practices easier, and help us to make them work.

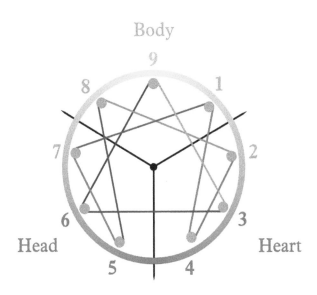

Head/Heart/Body Centers

We all have qualities from all of the centers, just as we all have all of the instincts, and characteristics from all of the personality styles. Think in terms of which do you use most often.

Your Enneagram style is assigned a number within one of these centers to provide you with additional information about the way you function. As with any system, you will find different people with many theories. In this application, let's keep it simple though.

A generalization on my part is that the first or lowest number in each section is other-oriented, the middle number is self-forgetting, and the highest number is self-oriented:

- ➤ **Heart Center Styles:**
  - ○ Helper/Giver (2) is other focused, looking for human connection, longs to know that they are loved. They hope to have positive feedback to show that they are loved. Their intention originates in the heart. To heal they must connect to their own heart and needs and practice loving themselves.
  - ○ Achiever/Performer (3) is task focused, losing themselves in the job, but when they focus on working through their heart, instead of their own need, they become great mentors and well-admired leaders. Their healing happens in the heart when they experience themselves as valuable instead of only seeing the value of what they do.
  - ○ Individualist (4) is most interested in how they feel in response to the idea/world etc. Since they are reactive to conformity, they are also known as rebels. Unlike 8s, who long to know they matter, the Individualist know they matter and want you to know they matter. They can be very emotional, and their healing comes when they can see the heart/feelings can be balanced with objectivity.
- ➤ **Head Center Styles:**
  - ○ Intellectual/Investigator (5) is information focused. Commonly in reaction to demands of the outer world, they use information from in their head as currency and to protect themselves from others' demands. Their healing comes when they find ways to relate to others in compassion, giving up mental arrogance caused by fear of needed things that they can't control.
  - ○ Loyal Skeptic (6) analyzes to keep themselves safe. Forgets self in the quest for community and justice, loyalty to xyz easily overtakes a sense of self. Their healing comes with self-loyalty and trust. Trusting that half the analysis is enough and having faith in their ability to make good choices for their lives.

- Enthusiast/Epicure (7) uses the mind to avoid the unpleasantness of the mundane. Can be lost in thought, their healing comes with accepting the world, grounding and embracing all parts of being human, when they learn to do or at least respect the things that make the world work.
- **Body Center Styles:**
  - Challenger/Influencers (8) long to matter in the world. They feel a visceral experience of being negated which make them "fight" that sense of being disregarded in the world. Need others to affirm their influence, will build and lead with gusto. To heal they need to be grateful, to stop fighting and see that they do matter in the world, even in small ways to put the sword and anger down and let love into the longing heart.
  - Peacemaker/Mediator (9) They are willing to forget themselves for the sake of peace around them. Wants to experience their inner world and enjoy the comfort of the body/material world. Their healing comes when they stop trying to control the world by neutralizing themselves. They find more peace saying their truth and cooperating in the world they have been trying to avoid.
  - Perfectionist/Reformer (1) they focus first on perfecting themselves, then the world around them.
- **Head Center Styles:**
  - Rely on thinking, data, analysis first.
  - Upside is clear thinking, practical application, problem-solving.
  - Downside is scattered, lost in the mental world, avoiding others. Can become anxious, hostile towards others.
    - Intellectual/Investigator (5): Attention toward the inner world of thoughts and information gathering.
    - Loyal Skeptic (6): Attention towards fairness, belonging, autonomy.

111

- Enthusiast/Epicure (7): Attention outwards, let's go, always more.

> **Heart Center Styles:**
  o Rely on emotional information first.
  o Upside is the heart, warm, caring, empowering, creating.
  o Downside is manipulation, out of balance either too emotional or too emotionally distant. Can be prideful or resent not having what they need.
    - Helper/Giver (2): Attention towards others, intuitive knowing of needs, emotional intelligence.
    - Achiever/Performer (3): Attention on getting things done.
    - Individualist (4): Attention towards own feelings, senses knowing.

> **Body Center Styles:**
  o Rely on gut, power, body language, knowing.
  o Upside is strength, leadership, protectors, fearlessness.
  o Downside is anger, rage, lack of faith in life, others, struggling to feel love, overpowering others.
    - Challenger/Influencers (8): Attention towards power over others, leads toward establishing their territory.
    - Peacemaker/Mediator (9): Attention towards the world, establishing a peaceful environment.
    - Perfectionist/Reformer (1): Attention towards making the world a perfect place.

Wings

You will find information on wings inside the sections for each style.

In some writing on the Enneagram, you will see people refer to themselves with their dominant wing, for example, I am a 2 with a 3 wing. It simply means that they identify more the qualities that influence them from that wing than the other.

I see that people use both of their wings to be successful in the world. If you are struggling or out of balance, try looking towards developing qualities and resources that you are not accessing from your wings.

Each style has wings, these are the types immediately to either side of their main type.

 ➢ Wings are the types next to your main style.
 ➢ These influence you but are not your main motivation.
 ➢ Wings help to balance us out. Think about the idea that some styles are more outward, more self-forgetting, or more inward. It is then a natural outcome of using our wings to bring us into more efficacy and balance.
 ➢ Think about the main style and then consider the wings on each side.
 ➢ The underlying motivation is the same, the execution and personality are influenced by how many qualities you use from each wing.
 ➢ All styles use both wings, but we tend to use one of them more often

Arrows

When you look at the Enneagram you will see that there are lines that connect each style with two other styles that are not their wings.

Over the many years of Enneagram development people have looked at the system, it becomes clear that each style had these connections.

In some writing, you will find these referred to as growth or stress arrows. Meaning that in some points of view, one is seen as lower functioning and one as a positive.

Over the years there has been an adjustment in the thinking on this, and I am glad for this change. The more current idea is that our arrows give us access to qualities that can be found in either thriving or stressed behavior.

For example, as a Challenger/Influencer, my arrows are Giver/Helper and Intellectual/Investigator. In the old method, it says that I advance as a person when I use the softness and connection of the Helper/Giver. This is true, but to say that I only have growth or positives is not accurate. I have experienced myself in the dark side of the Helper/Giver, and it was profoundly bad for me.

Further, the old way says that for me stress is found in the Intellectual/Investigator. I can get a bit lost in too much data, but one of my best places is to find joy in a life of learning. The dark side of the Intellectual/Investigator is to fear people, to project negativity onto the world and go into isolation.

Yes, I agree that our arrows play key roles in the way we move around in our lives, but I am more inclined to say that both the up and downside are available to us. Examine the arrows and wings to see more nuance about our inner working is a smart way to expand your understanding of you.

It is a fun way to connect with others because ultimately, we all connect somewhere. Build those bridges through wings and arrows too!

The 9 Styles of the Enneagram

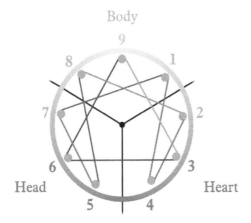

About each style:

Perfectionist/Reformer (1)

Helper/Giver (2)

Achiever/Performer (3)

Romantic/Individualist (4)

Intellectual/Investigator

Loyal Skeptic (6)

Enthusiast/Epicure (7)

Challenger/Influencer (8)

Peacemaker/Mediator (9)

Thriving vs Surviving

Introduction

Maslow's Hierarchy

Graphics of each style

Motivations that Drives Each Style

- Perfectionist/Reformer (1)
    - If I am perfect, I will be loved. It is my job to manifest the perfect world that I see as possible.
- Helper/Giver (2)
    - I need to love and feel loved. I will do everything possible to make this happen.
- Achiever/Performer (3)
    - I need to feel valued. I am valued based on what I achieve.
- Romantic/Individualist (4)
    - Feeling deeply and being unique gives life meaning.
- Intellectual/Investigator (5)
    - I love my mind, it energizes me, my inner world is very nourishing while people are often tiresome.
- Loyal Skeptic (6):
    - I need to have faith, to feel safe, to learn trust. Once I put my trust in you, I am your knight.
- Enthusiast/Epicure (7):
    - I don't want to miss anything. There is so much more than I can take in and it's important not to let life pass you by.
- Challenger/Influencer (8):
    - I need to know that I matter. It is important to have validation and place in the world.
- Peacemaker/Mediator (9)
    - I see and feel many things in the world around me, what I want is to quiet the chaos out there – to feel inner peace.

Upsides for each style:

- Perfectionist/Reformer (1)
  - I am dedicated, a very hard worker, accurate, detailed, capable, I can possess a great deal of personal power while being caring to those around me.
- Helper/Giver (2)
  - I am excellent at accessing and meeting complex needs. I am a great person to put in a situation where emotional intelligence is important. I don't let people down.
- Achiever/Performer (3)
  - I know how to get things done. I can see efficient paths to success. When I am in my heart, I can be an excellent mentor.
- Romantic/Individualist (4)
  - I am creative, innovative, and set high standards. Life is my art. I am fierce in the face of difficult emotions.
- Intellectual/Investigator (5)
  - I work in the intellectual depths, thrive on research, philosophy and mental complexity. I am mentally diligent.
- Loyal Skeptic (6)
  - I love being with the group and enjoying experiences. Once you have earned my trust, I am passionately loyal. My analytical skills help me assure a good result.
- Enthusiast/Epicure (7)
  - I am upbeat and high energy, with a great capability for rallying the group. I love getting people to think progressively.
- Challenger/Influencer (8)
  - I embrace leadership, you can count on me to look out for the team, to protect my people, to reward those who are loyal to me and our cause. I am very loving under the big exterior.
- Peacemaker/Mediator (9)
  - I am very intuitive, feeling the unifying force of the Universe. I am much more powerful than people can usually see because I try to stay very even-keeled.

9 Styles – Actions

- ➤ Perfectionist/Reformer (1)
  - o Accept excellence over perfection.
  - o See the beauty in yourself and others, avoid criticizing.
- ➤ Helper/Giver (2)
  - o Put your own wellbeing in balance with the rest of the world.
  - o Respect other's boundaries.
  - o Preserve some energy for yourself.
- ➤ Achiever/Performers (3)
  - o Stop and see the humanity and life around you.
  - o Use moving meditation and practice softening your heart.
- ➤ Romantic/Individualist (4)
  - o Focus on emotional balance. Affirm your own uniqueness.
  - o Accept reality, respect the practical.
- ➤ Intellectual/Investigator (5)
  - o Put your intelligence into the world, wisdom comes from the doing of the application of information.
  - o Embrace your own human self and that of others.
- ➤ Loyal Skeptic (6)
  - o Find balance in your need to analyze.
  - o See that you have made successful choices helps you relax.
- ➤ Enthusiast/Epicure (7)
  - o Gratitude for all you have will help you to stop searching.
  - o Pair down, eliminating non-essentials.
- ➤ Challenger/Influencer (8)
  - o Embrace your vulnerability.
  - o Make a point of looking for the ways people are your allies.
  - o Check yourself if you are creating tense situations.
- ➤ Peacemaker/Mediator (9)
  - o Schedule non-active or indulgent times where you are honoring your desire for peace, quiet and nurturing things.
  - o Use this time to journal and reflect on your inner world.

About the Perfectionist/Reformer (1)

live with a massive inner critic; a few words of even constructive criticism feel like a lot to me! Make sure that you are putting the criticism into perspective. Not sugarcoating, but also not overstating it.

For me, helping you improve is a supportive action.

Delegating is difficult, I can only give my work to someone I know will do a great job with it!

I like clear specific goals. If you give me directions trust me to get it done, I may be a micromanager, but I hate being micromanaged.

I have a great sense of humor, help me relax, and you will get to enjoy it.

I am worth listening to, I hope people see how much I care.

I get tired of people thinking I am tiresome.

It makes me nervous when people I care about don't follow the rules and implement best practices, I am afraid bad things will happen to them.

Through meeting the most stringent standards I find serenity.

Perfection has a sacred quality.

I will never shirk my responsibility.

I have a duty to be an example for those around me.

I can see exactly the perfect way to live; I am willing to work tirelessly to reform things to match my vision.

If things are not done with exact standards, bad things occur.

I am feeling, but not sentimental and hate spending a lot of time wallowing in emotion.

A story about the Perfectionist/Reformer (1)

My friend Eric D. is a Perfectionist/Reformer. I know him through his wonderful fiancé, soon to be wife, Jen, who is a Helper/Giver.

When you first meet him, he is hard to read because he holds himself in relaxed attention, or maybe it's that he is relaxed when he is at attention. Hearing he was in the military makes sense. He is alert. Even after a few beers, in his relaxed state, he likely notices more than most people.

He is a good match for my Helper/Giver friend because he is a kindhearted person. His Helper/Giver wing shows up in that he is willing to help, and perhaps enjoys the connections and sense of purpose. He has a generous spirit, though if you were to be aggressive with him, I imagine that you would find him a formidable opponent. He has that centered physical power that Perfectionist/Reformer hold when they are in a healthy place. His body language says he can back up what he thinks. He is willing to sacrifice for his beliefs, finding a selfless power to make things better than he found them. He supports and encourages the betterment of the people around him.

His job gives him the chance to travel and have a wide sphere of social connections and influence. He is helpful to the offices, while he pushes himself to get things right and helps to hold people to high standards.

His Peacemaker/Mediator wing makes it clear that he doesn't want conflict, he just wants to enjoy things being right in the world. The driving he does between the regional offices gives him time to unwind in his own little neat, clean, well-cared for world. He needs that time to retreat and have a break in a place that is under his control.

At home, he is the man with the neatly edged lawn, the fence with boards that are not warped, and helps keep the house in good order because it makes both he and his mate more at ease. He is appreciative of the kindness and directness that Jen expresses herself with, unafraid to hear her truth, not good at guessing, but feels comfortable with no-nonsense information that he can implement to show he is on her side.

Tools for the Perfectionist/Reformer (1)

➤ Take a step back, notice that you are a whole person.
➤ Perfect is not exact. It actually doesn't exist.
  o Everyone's perfect is different.
  o The perfect idea in your head is not ideal for everyone.
  o Excellent is a better goal, you can get to excellent.
  o Perfect is not healthy because it causes you to struggle. It is subjective, and your "inner critic or inner saboteur" will use it to keep you from feeling at easy in the world. It will keep moving your target and you will have no fun or rest.
  o Good enough, excellent, and ish (darn close) are your best strategies for a better quality of life.
➤ Breathe into your body, into the heart, and all the way down into the earth.
  o Knowing that you are a whole person and not the sum of perfect parts helps you to be kinder to yourself.
  o Be in touch with your emotions. Don't wallow, but also avoid repressing.
  o Use exercise as a time to go inward, to show respect to your more complex creative, feeing side. This will calm what can become rage if ignored.
➤ Let go of everything else and notice that you are whole, safe, you are a miracle just as you are, you are entitled to rest and feel good.
➤ Notice that you are better when you don't try quite so hard.
➤ Excellence is better than perfect because it is achievable!
➤ Assess the love that exists in your life.
➤ Focus on things that do work and be grateful for them.
➤ Allow others to learn what you already know and allow yourself the pleasure of learning from them.
➤ Make time to enjoy your sense of humor.
➤ *Self-Compassion + Acceptance of reality = More Experience of Pleasure*

121

Perfectionist/Reformer (1) Wings

Perfectionist/Reformer (1) w/Peacemaker/Mediator (9) wing

- Considerate of others.
- See and seek the ideal.
- More inward.
- Self-protective.
- Acts based on values.
- Stern.
- Judgmental.
- Distant.

Perfectionist/Reformer (1) w/Helper/Giver (2) wing

- A good person.
- Seek to benefit the world.
- Takes care of others.
- Denies own needs.
- More outward.
- More compassionate.
- Wants to educate about what is right.
- Connecting.

Perfectionist/Reformer (1) Arrows

Use traits from style Enthusiast/Epicure (7):

- Take care of yourself.
- You can't make things perfect, that is not possible.
- You are safe even with the imperfections of life.
- Try to remember that others don't see things the way you do, and their point of view is important too.
- It is not perfect to try to be perfect, it is impossible and not compassionate.
- It's important for life to be fun!

Use traits from style Romantic/Individualist (4):

- Emotions happen, if you are feeling angry – pay attention to your inner world.
- Allow time for creative things.
- Look for beauty.
- If you feel self-righteous, or overly critical, take a break and change your approach.
- Watch out for the way you put your expectations on others.

About the Helper/Giver (2)

> - I enjoy seeing others be happy.
> - It makes me feel good to know that I am contributing.
> - It makes me feel awesome (no matter how I blush or protest) when people appreciate me for my efforts.
> - I have pride, but I don't like to have to stand up for myself. I like it when people show up for me, the way I show up for them.
> - Relating and connecting are priorities, success in business is related to relationships that produce great results.
> - It is a bad idea to neglect, abuse or take advantage of my good nature, I can become resentful when hurt.
> - Count on me to make the team join forces, I understand people, but it's not easy to speak up – it's important that you make time to listen to me. I believe that if I connect with people and meet their needs, they will love me.
> - I am concerned that I am not lovable. I try not to bother others with my needs.
> - Angry people scare me. It is upsetting when people don't respond to kindness. On the other hand, when I am neglected long enough, I can become very mean, bitter or resentful.
> - If we are all just a little nicer to each other, things will go better.
> - There are people in need, and it is our job to make sure that I/we take care of them.
> - If I help others, the world will be a better place.
> - Relationships are the foundation for success.
> - Positive feedback drives me towards success!

A Story About a Helper/Giver (2)

LaRea came to me as a client a few years ago. She is a great example of Helper/Giver using her strengths to build a successful career.

You feel the Helper/Giver in her from the first moment you speak with her. Her Texas accent, the smile in her voice, the genuine concern for people, and her conviction to an ethical code of the "right way to treat each other" greet you, and you are in love with her before you know it.

This woman has the sort of determination that would make any girl from Texas proud. LaRea made her way into and through the Self-Funded Insurance Industry. At the height of her leadership career she ran a company with 167 employees. She has held multiple board positions in her industry including high ranking positions with: HCAA, SPBA, and TPBA. She has worked successfully in training, sales, and operations. I dare say everyone from her clients to her staff have felt her personal concern and interest along with her high standards and ability to achieve her goals/lead her to team to reach their goals.

All that means that this 5'2", Helper/Giver drew on a lot of her inner strength. To lead with heart is a challenge, but when it is done, the leader is truly loved and has what become a loyal community instead of staff.

She clearly knew how to put people at ease and cared about the care and service they received, she also has the Perfectionist/Reformer keen eye for accuracy. She didn't stop there, not this girl, using her Achiever wing constantly moved up until she found herself running the place.

If you take a look at how she uses the energy from her arrows, she drew on the energy of the Challenger for those times when she had to push through things and her Individualist arrow because she loves crafting.

It's been a pleasure to work with her. Her biggest challenge was not surprising: not to let people who behaved badly effect how she felt about herself. Her favorite quote from our work together is:

"Other people's bad behavior is not about me!"

Tools for The Giver/Helper (2)

- ➤ Take care of yourself.
- ➤ Ask yourself, what do I need? How do I feel?
- ➤ Tell others when you need help, and ask for them to show up for you.
  - o Others can't see what you need the same way you can see what they need. It's not that they don't care, it's that they don't see the same way, but are usually happy to ask when you let them know how they can show up for you.
- ➤ Put down thoughts about what other's needs. Trust that they will be ok without you.
  - o You do not have to sacrifice yourself to connect. Some sacrifice is compassionate, too much and you are doing their job for them. Which is counterproductive.
- ➤ Sometimes thinks about whether you are really helping.
  - o Is it possible you are interfering with their process?
  - o Are you controlling them or the situation?
  - o Are you in their space instead of paying attention to yourself?
- ➤ Tell people what you need and how you feel.
  - o Be aware that, without meaning to, you can become manipulative. Therefore, it is so important that you know and express your needs.
  - o Unmet needs become resentment and manipulating to get attention. To heal the neglect.
- ➤ Make sure you have a few different people that are close friends.
  - o You need a lot of human contact, sometimes you need a bunch of best friends to satisfy your capacity to connect.
- ➤ Sometimes it is fun to have relationships that are about mutual interests or playing, be careful to avoid relationships based on you giving too much.
- ➤ Embrace power! You have a lot of loving energy; the world needs you to stand tall and show us all that connecting, and caring is powerful!
- ➤ *Love is Powerful + Self Compassion = Greater Capacity to Love*

Helper/Giver (2) Wings

Helper/Giver (2) using Perfectionist/Reformer (1)

- Seeks to give of self.
- Feels a strong sense of purpose.
- "If I am good enough you will love me."
- It is very difficult to say no.
- Can be confusing when they are both caring and judging.
- Judges self for own needs-rejects self.

Helper/Giver (2) using Achiever/Performer (3)

- Love people, being around them, helping them, building things together!
- Affectionate.
- Self-assured.
- Image-conscious.
- Intuitive.
- Manipulative.
- Forgets own feelings.

Helper/Giver (2) Arrow

Use traits from style Individualist/Romantic (4)

➢ Engage in the beauty of expression.
➢ Careless about how others need you to be and more about how you want to be.
➢ You love being eloquent.
➢ Accept without embarrassment of admiration for yourself.
➢ Give yourself time.

Use traits from style Challenger/Influencer (8)

➢ Understand power as a part of life.
➢ Learn to use the ideal of empowering rather than seeking power over others.
➢ When people are aggressive with you, it is your job to show them how to treat another person.
➢ Your strength empowers others to take good care of themselves.

About the Achiever/Performer (3)

- Getting things done matters – a lot!
- Ultimately, I am hoping to find love, to find what is holy. This is why I work so hard.
- I get lost in the needs of the project and forget myself, and other people.
  - But I don't lose track of my image, I need to be impressive.
- Achievers like leadership and management positions because it gives them the opportunity to always have a next project. Significant others complain about feeling "not as important." If you are dealing with an Achiever who is not functioning very well, you are probably not being treated very well.
- Achievers struggle with personal relationships until they emotionally mature and recognize that they need people around that they love.
- Achiever really like praise.
  - To help me out: affirm me when I do things that are human, empowering, and kind. I am a heart person, and I like being reconnected to my own heart.
- I can be a very empowering person. I love it when I can see that I am helping others to succeed. This is a sign that I am emotionally thriving.
- Ask me for my input, my advice, I am very capable and love to contribute to success. Acknowledge me for my assistance.
- I need to remember that kindness and gentleness are powerful tools.
- My appearance is very important. I want to avoid being judged.
- I need to be respected.
- Let me lead this show, my way is good!
- It is painful when people dismiss me or don't listen to me.
- I am an outstanding, effective person!
- People win when they do things my way.
- I have this nagging feeling inside. Fear of failure looms in my mind.

131

A Story About the Achiever Performer (3)

Achiever/Performers are not likely to come to people like me for help. When they do, it is unlikely that they are willing to let their peers know they did. Below is a story about an Achiever/Performer (not his real name).

William had moved up in his company with success after success, in a glorious rise to the top. He didn't want to show his pride, but the pleasure of his achievement was like a parade that entered the room ahead of him.

His wife was exhausted by a long list of his behavior that showed her his lack of interest in the family. She had given up her career to raise the family and his arrogance was distasteful to the point that she did not want him to touch her. He was always busy, working, traveling but couldn't relax at home and be with them.

He was exhausted of not being appreciated at home, of not being touched and wondering why everyone but his wife thought he was awesome.

It was the lack of intimacy that drove him for help. It's good he reached out. Often, the pressure of driving yourself to perform without feeling loved is the sort of stress that leads to illness or breakdown.

The change was a bit slow because the world rewarded him for his money and accomplishments. He discovered warmth and laughter when he learned to just hang with his boys. Over time he learned to let his wife see him as a real vulnerable person and to be caring about her feelings instead of defending himself. Learning to see and appreciate his wife more than his accomplishments repaired the marriage and he now has increasing intimacy instead of a divorce settlement.

It was very important to reinforce that he could still achieve what made him happy while he and his family all gave and received positive attention simply because they love each other.

His heart softened and he still rocks it at work. He is now an even more effective leader because he is happier and works on being compassionate.

Tools for the Achiever/Performer (3)

- ➤ You are not your work!
  - o Think about what is wonderful about being alive that has nothing to do with work.
    - Do you love the taste of certain comfort food?
    - Want to tell your sweetheart that you love them?
    - Ask someone about themselves and stay with it until you see and feel them as a person.
- ➤ You are not your image!
  - o Use your Individualist wing and do something crazy.
  - o It is really good for you to goof off.
  - o Wear something different, something that makes you a little afraid of being judged. Enjoy playfulness.
- ➤ It is time to pay attention to your feelings.
  - o Not just your passions like money and accomplishment, but feeling love for someone, something, and your own life just because!
- ➤ Find activities that don't involve work, that have nothing to do with image. Camp, get dirty, be silly, intentionally go along with someone's idea, and decide to find some positives.
- ➤ Choose not to compete: Instead, when you have a chance intentionally give your help to others.
- ➤ There is a time to charge the hill, and a time to meditate, a time to be impressive, and a time to be! Don't lose your edge, do indulge other points of view looking for points of agreement and connection.
- ➤ Rest and relax. Try picking up hobbies or things you enjoyed in your youth. Try things you have "always wanted to do but have been too busy".
- ➤ Use short meditations or quiet periods to give your feelings and inner world attention.
- ➤ Trust that emotional intelligence won't slow you down.
- ➤ *Self-Compassion + Intention Awareness of Others Value = Purpose*

133

Achiever/Performer (3) Wings

Achiever/Performer (3) w/Helper/Giver (2) Wing

- ➤ Very socially capable, connections make things happen.
- ➤ Show their feelings more easily.
- ➤ Can lose themselves in the charm game.
- ➤ Driven towards success.
- ➤ Can be empowering to others.
- ➤ Need to prove self/value.
- ➤ Can become entitled.
- ➤ Can become nasty and arrogant when not shown appreciation.

Achiever/Performer (3) w/Individual/Romantic (4) Wing

- ➤ Focus more on being professional.
- ➤ Image is both individual and sleek.
- ➤ Quality of work is the key factor.
- ➤ More in touch with own feelings, while not disinterested in others, more interested in work and self.
- ➤ Self-worth is intensely connected to work.
- ➤ Can become emotionally variable.
- ➤ Can be unrealistic about their demands or projects.

Achiever/Performer (3) Arrows

Use traits from style Peacemaker/Mediator (9)

> ➢ Increases sense of emotional stability.
> ➢ Creates caring about people while maintaining sense of purpose.
> ➢ Helps the 3 relax, take recreation time.
> ➢ Reduces identity with the world's opinion, increases personal well-being.
> ➢ 3s give themselves some time to take care of themselves, to reflect.

Use traits from style Loyal Skeptic (6)

> ➢ Increases attention to detail.
> ➢ Increases loyalty to a larger cause.
> ➢ Balances need to "be on top".
> ➢ Increases mindfulness.
> ➢ Puts goals in perspective.

About the Romantic/Individualist (4)

- I feel things very deeply, without fear of feeling.
- Resisting being "like someone else" it drives Romantic/Individualist to push the edges of what has been done.
  - Therefore, they thrive as creatives.
  - Think of the musician Prince who woke up our sense and pushed us with his music, his style, his being, challenged us to consider our self-imposed limits, and not allow the mundane to swallow us so easily.
- Romantics can become obsessed with emotion, it is a form of exploring their inner world.
- This can be a creative boon to a company or a group. Bringing a wealth of artistic insight that few other styles offer.
- If the Romantic has not learned to manage the emotions or created an outlet, being around them can feel overwhelming. It can be hard to relate to a person who is so lost in their ideas and feelings.
- 4s can become distant from people who don't "understand them".
- If they don't experience success in life, they risk becoming isolated.
- They can become arrogant as they believe they are "better than others" who focus on the boring mundane things of the world.
- I am sensitive and unique. I feel things others miss.
- The world is boring to the Romantic, so they create.
  - In the best cases they create and open our minds.
  - In the worst they create fantasy that consumes them.
- Why do others have so much more than I do? I want to be functional. I must work at it. When I get the functional part down, I am very successful in life.
- I long to feel what is Holy.
- Often found in artistic fields, the world counts on me to shake life up.
- Accepting my emotion and hold a sacred place for me to enter the world to support me in finding objectivity about my emotions.

A Story About the Romantic/Individualist (4)

Charise drew her languid arm across her body. He poignantly shook his head holding her stocking in his hand as it draped across his leg and hers. Suspended in the air like a shimmering reminder of the dashed hopes for the evening. The ring box in his pocket was outlined against his leg. He adored her and would try again, but does she know that he loves her so deeply while she lets old hurts tear jagged ruts in her heart?

He had planned a lovely meal, but at dinner, her former lover was to sit a at able across from them. He had left her, and it was always a knife in her to feel the unrequited love she carried for him. Tonight's carefully planned marriage proposal was to be preempted by her disdain for him.

Her dressing gown was collapsed on the ground as she was no longer in it. She noticed it's lack of form, mentally rode the edge of satin. Her finger was brushing her lip wondering what the edge of the robe would feel like.

He brought her back to the room with a groan. She was emotionally spent. He looked at her and said, "what happened?"

"He came in and stabbed me in the heart", "You drank far too much, and I can't bear the idea of making love to you in that state. It makes you distracted. I see you evaporate. You say you love me, yet you can't stand to see and hear my stories if they aren't pretty!"

In the above scene you have a glimpse into the world of a Romantic individualist. While they can be volatile, emotional, they are sensuous, time with them is rich.

They can't tolerate emotional insincerity and you won't get away with it. They may allow themselves their dramas, but they will be rooted in what the Romantic feels in their truth. They will process emotion with you. They can't not process emotion and you will join if you want to be close to them.

Imagine living in an inner world that is so full, yet needing with all your might to individuate from the status quo of the world that you abhor.

Tools for the Romantic/Individualist (4)

Make time for practical things. You need to make time and space to connect with the outer world.

➤ Practice gratitude to help you balance your darker emotional thoughts with positive thoughts and experience.
➤ Respect others success. Pay attention to the good that comes from order and putting effort into the practical areas of life.
➤ Look for the beauty, individuality, and value in creative projects that aren't "your thing". Give others the respect you want.
➤ Spend time practicing being objective about emotions. Compassionately putting them "in their place" so you have room for other experiences.
  o Your emotions are not you. If you are possessed by emotion, you need help to become engaged in the world and objective about your emotions.
  o You will judge others for being mundane, not feeling, but you can become so caught up in your emotions that you dehumanize them. Wake up to what is running you.
➤ Expand your experiences in the world and be disciplined about moving your attitude towards acceptance of life and others. Be cautious about complaining.
  o It is wonderful to practice your uniqueness, you must also question what you are sacrificing to be so different.
    ▪ Are you pushing away people who love you?
    ▪ Are you missing the mark on self-care? Some Romantics swim off in their body of emotions, creating a world for themselves to languish in and missing out on the good stuff of life.
➤ It is a critical need for you to schedule creative time.
➤ *Embrace the Practical + Gratitude = Upward Movement*

Individualist/Romanic (4) Wings

Romantic/Individualist (4) w/Achiever/Performer (3) wing

- ➢ Ambitious.
- ➢ Creative.
- ➢ Emotional.
- ➢ Deep thinking, philosophical.
- ➢ Image-conscious.
- ➢ Can hide their emotions well.
- ➢ Need attention, affirmation of their value.
- ➢ Success = my chosen audience loves me.
- ➢ Failure = Self contempt.

Romantic/Individualist (4) w/Intellectual/Investigator (5) wing

- ➢ Individualist, pushing limits.
- ➢ Proving self.
- ➢ Needs to be admired for uniqueness.
- ➢ Excited by their own specialness.
- ➢ Can be very dark and emotional.
- ➢ Can bring art and science together.
- ➢ Can reject social norms.

Individualist/Romanic (4) Arrows

Use traits from style Perfectionist/Reformer (1)

➤ When 4's use the traits from 1s to find balance and equanimity, they come into functional action.
➤ 4s paying attention to the details of what it takes to accomplish things makes them grateful.
➤ Appreciation for action, respect for the real world lifts the 4 up.

Use traits from style Helper/Giver (2)

➤ When 4s care about others they can use this to balance out their emotional highs and lows.
➤ When 4s get overly involved in other people's emotions they get caught on the roller coaster of feelings with them and lose their balance.
➤ It is upsetting for the individualist to feel obligated regarding other people's feelings.

About the Intellectual/Investigator (5)

- They feel the world is demanding.
  - I feel drained when I have to process all the meaningless data that is present in a crowd.
  - Unless I am studying the crowd and mining for data that interests me.
  - I can enjoy social engineering, matching up people to see how things go. That further takes the social pressure off of me.
- 5s engage in knowledge as a way to manage the chaos in the world around them.
  - I set high intellectual standards. Because to me, the data is a living thing, researching ideas and topics opens up the world. This allows me to create mini worlds inside of my main world and have control over them, it also it gives me ability to corelate data, to see things in my head and then look at them.
- Intellectuals can have a powerful sense of humor.
- Many are gamers, and leaders in the technology industry.
- They can be very intense and enjoy the power of heavy metal music and the art of classical music equally. They are usually very observant, even if they keep what they see to themselves.
- Emotions are not the realm of the 5. The mind and thoughts are.
- With extremely active minds the 5 literally has the need for information.
- As long as they balance this need with the rest of their needs.
- It is amusing when people know what they are talking about.
- Mental jousting is energizing. It is so boring when people take our jousts personally.
- People are too sensitive.
- I don't understand why they feel bad when I tell them with enthusiasm about why their idea won't work. It's science.
  - People are not very smart.

143

A Story About the Intellectual/Investigator (5):

A colleague, let's call him Lamar, has a sharp and perfectly dry wit that I enjoy. There is no end to the droll observations and comments he makes.

I give him space, letting him lead most of the time, as he is the one who feels a great need to monitor his energy. He hates (literally) when people feel they can interrupt him. He enjoys snacks, conversations, and friendships that are given with no attachment. He is overwhelmed by too much. It's like he is uncomfortable with needing much from the world.

He belonged to online forums before social media was a thing. His mind absorbs data and enjoys research, he usually has a good answer to most questions or knows where to get it.

Once a month or so, I will invite him for coffee or when he is ready to talk, he says, "let's have coffee." I almost always say yes. I had to learn his need for quiet time inside his own mind time is not about me at all.

Our conversations are always rich and rewarding. Never gossipy or trite, always some deep conversation about ideas, solutions and it's so very genuine. Never fluffy. Always an experience of new ideas.

When I need to know something, I send him an email: text and phoning him are intrusive. He is knowledgeable or will find things I never could about a subject, so treat him with the respect of an old wise person and let him tell me what he knows. I am not a mentally lazy person, I just really appreciate the way his mind works, and he enjoys being respected for the assets he controls.

When I want to know how he is doing, I ask him what he is studying or what's new, and sometimes just ask him without flourish about what's going on for him. There are few with whom he will personally share, so I feel happy we have made this bond. It started when I broke the ice with a joke.

Don't go to him for empathy, go for answers.

If he gives me a compliment, he really means it. I treasure it.

Tools for the Intellectual/Investigator (5)

➢ Make the effort to be aware of your needs and act on your own behalf.
  o Also, ask others to help you.
➢ Express about yourself. Not just what you know.
  o You are a whole person with emotions. You will be happier and healthier when you treat yourself according to reality.
  o No matter how much you act like you need no one or nothing, when you admit you do and establish that your needs can be met you will enjoy life more.
  o Learn to cook, it is a great methodical way to meet your needs, enjoy sensation, have a conversation, meet people and share yourself without exposing too much until you trust them.
➢ It is ok to have an opinion that is based on emotion.
  o Everything does not have to be scientifically proven. It's ok to have impulses and bring emotion into your decision process.
➢ Lean into life. Volunteer or join a group that does something you enjoy. Just for fun is good enough.
➢ Even if you meet online, go be around people. Roll playing games and game nights are a great way to meet people like you.
➢ Enroll in classes, go to a place to be with people and learn.
➢ Respect your body and it's needs. Make time and space for your body to enjoy life; nature, massages, and comfortable surroundings help you relax.
➢ Take risks in relationships. Test the waters and notice that you are safe interacting.
➢ Make some of your alone or study time about high concepts, matters of the heart, spiritual practice, etc. Perhaps make a study of the higher qualities of energy.
➢ Get exercise and build strength.
  o You get depleted easily. Build your reserves.
➢ *Moving Outwards + Appreciating different types of people = Connection*

Intellectual/Investigator (5) Wings

Intellectual/Investigator (5) w/ Romantic/Individualist (4) wing

➤ Philosophy meets art creating a person who is emotional and overthinks.
➤ Generally withdrawn into a world of their own making.
➤ Looking for something that they have idealized inside of themselves.
➤ Genius can arise from this or dark unfulfilled longing.

Intellectual/Investigator (5) w/Loyal Skeptic (6) wing

➤ Tend towards intense mental gymnastics.
➤ Can research and analyze with great pleasure.
➤ Generally, want to do something good for the world without being overly involved with people.
➤ Enjoys creative, humorous pursuits.
➤ Naturally suspicious they can oppose authority.
➤ Private, can develop paranoia if isolated.

Investigator/Intellectual (5) Arrows

Use traits from style Enthusiast/Epicure (7)

➢ A positive way that 5s can use 7 qualities is to expand their thoughts about people and things.
➢ Try new things.
➢ Not take things so seriously.
➢ Make the effort to be friendlier and more outgoing.
➢ Enjoy play.

Use traits from style Challenger/Influencer (8)

➢ When 5s access their 8 qualities, they are in their bodies, feeling purposeful.
➢ They leave behind the withdrawn quality of the average 5 and enjoy a boldness that energizes them.
➢ 5s let themselves go into the world, they educate us and confront misinformation.

About the Loyal Skeptic (6)

> Loyal Skeptics analyze everything. Their minds see detailed patterns and can project possible outcomes with ease.

> They are often very compassionate though objective about it.

> Because they see things that could help or hurt others and they are very interested in the well-being of the tribe, they put an effort into making things good for the group.

> 6s rarely put themselves in the light of being more important than others, but they do hold their own methods in very high esteem.

> Belonging to the group that they personally feel is trustworthy matters to them.

> 6s test people, relationships, situations, to see if the others in the world "out there" are trustworthy.

> Their deepest desire is to be safe. To feel at ease in their own mind.

> They fear dependence on something "out there".

> I want to be my own authority.

> I may be loyal to you, but you don't own me.

> You can trust me. I am a rock and would put my life down before I betray my word.

> I am a craftsperson at heart.

> I value the dedication, focus, and effort it takes to perform a task in an excellent way.

> It is hard to deal with my own feelings. I shut down or become angry when you pry.

> I have a hard time hearing I was wrong because I am very hard on myself.

> It is hard to move forward on decisions that require commitment because my word means so much, once I've said "yes, I will do that" there is pressure to never let anyone down.

A Story About the Loyal Skeptic (6)

Margaret was a friend of mine, she sat at the reception desk and I was behind her as the A/R clerk. She was in her 60s and I in my 20s, but we had the common experience of being raised in the Catholic Church, of having a sort of irreverent sense of humor, and we hoped the world would be a better place.

She was sweet. Had a great faith in God that had led her to become a nun early in her life but had a great insecurity about everything in the world around her.

She was caught in the 1980s changes in the church. Her order was closing its' convent. She along with a few others had to go get normal jobs and a small apartment to help the order. For a woman in her sixties who had lived in a convent, this was very upsetting to her anxiety. The panic attacks of her young life had been calmed by the security of the convent, by the faith that was unchallenged and the order of her life.

Being thrown into the world where she faced not only the daunting number of choices, she had no experience in making on a daily basis. Living around people with different faiths or no faith was shaking her.

She was friendly, compassionate, and delightful, not very skillful about how things worked in the world, but eager to be part of the group, and find ways to "use her smarts" to contribute.

It was impossible for her to not worry about germs in the bathroom of the little office. She increasingly worried about things that she could not control and began seeing a counselor to help her cope with life's chaos.

As a Loyal Skeptic, she was facing a real crisis. She lost the security of the life she had been dedicated to. Her superiors eventually had her come to do work in the church where she could find emotional ease.

At the time I wasn't using the Enneagram, but in retrospect, Margaret shows us the dedicated and hardworking Loyal Skeptic. She was a delight, brought fairness and kindness, but struggled with the pace of life.

Tools for the Loyal Skeptic (6)

- ➤ Try to build trust with others.
  - o Notice the ways that they do show up for you.
  - o Notice ways that people who seem different on the surface still hold the same human needs and hope as you do.
  - o Your fear can dehumanize you and others. Instead of letting yourself get fearful of others, make a choice to not dehumanize, to avoid judgement, to see that you are safe.
  - o Avoid complaining or grumbling, it's a sign of destress.
- ➤ Use your vast capacity for compassion to do kind and useful actions, but don't overdo it and burn out. Then you get bitter.
- ➤ You have a very good mind, provided you give yourself positive challenges throughout life.
- ➤ Meditation for head types is best done with a focal point, you won't relate to a quiet mind, you will find a quieter mind if you focus and avoid chasing your thoughts around.
- ➤ Being human is imperfect, no one can stand up to the most stringent standards because we are all flawed.
  - o There has to be space for mistakes.
  - o Space for mistakes relieves some of the judgement that can result from analysis paralysis.
- ➤ Isolation is dangerous, human beings need each other.
- ➤ Pick a few different friends to talk with about private matters.
- ➤ Having a counselor is very helpful to have control over who knows what about you.
- ➤ Give yourself time to explore things that help your body relax, and help you feel aware of your body.
- ➤ Make a study of something that is amusing to you. Have a hobby that entertains you.
- ➤ Take time to assess who is kind, loving and respectful. Let them know that you appreciate them.
- ➤ *Trust you are safe + Play with Life = Inner Peace, Growth*

Loyal Skeptic (6) Wings

Loyal Skeptic (6) w/Intellectual Investigator 5 wing

➤ Protective of "their people".
➤ Egalitarian.
➤ Insists on independence but forgets to be human.
➤ Can become defensive and blaming.
➤ Wants to belong, to be the buddy.
➤ Uses humor to avoid feelings.
➤ Cheers the underdog.
➤ Can be very oppositional.
➤ Can become pessimistic, anxious.

Loyal Skeptic (6) w/Enthusiast/Epicure 7 wing

➤ Looks for friendship, wants to be accepted/liked.
➤ Playful, pleasure-seeking.
➤ Adventurous.
➤ Identifies with others' opinions of them.
➤ Dedicated and loyal.
➤ Can struggle with self-starting.
➤ Can become paralyzed with fear/anxious.

Loyal Skeptic (6) Arrows

Use Traits from Style Achiever/Performer (3)

> 6s can benefit from the 3s qualities of setting priorities to get to the goal.
> When the 6 uses positive aspects of the 3 they are more image conscious and extroverted.
> Feelings and awareness of other people's needs are 3 qualities that bring about a more energized quality.
> The confidence of the 3 reduces their anxiety.

Use Traits from Style Peacemaker / Meditator (9)

> Accessing the broad perception of the 9 eases 6s normal state of alert.
> The feeling of inner peace that comes from being connected to their body lifts the mind of the 6.
> Taking a break from analyzing feels great!

- Enthusiasts live with verve!
- Think about Auntie Mime's famous quote: "life is a banquet and most poor suckers are starving to death." This is what it is like inside of their worlds.
- Constant motion, creative ideas, and endless experiences make the world of an enthusiast exciting and sometimes exhausting.
- Moving meditations are an excellent choice for Enthusiast because it helps keep mind and body in the same place. It grounds and centers them so they can move their ideas into the world.
- Since they are a Head Centered people having some routine that helps them be attentive to their whole self is good. Fortunately exercise and yoga is trendy, so they are likely to be going to class.
- 7s tend to be extremely independent or lead the fun. They have more energy than most people and are energized by the prospect of getting new boundaries to challenge and worlds to create or explore.
- 7s can struggle with feeling supported, this causes anxiety.
- 7s can become disconnected with their own feelings and needs, though they are busy attending to others, making plans, or dreaming about their next adventure.
- While most people are pain avoidant, Enthusiasts make art of avoiding emotional issues. They are always cheerful and full of energy but getting real could mean facing repressed issues.
- I need to keep on moving, let's not miss a thing!
- Life is amazing; endless adventures, smells, tastes, etc.
  - I want some of it all.
- New things are more interesting.
- It's nice to have things and people to count on, but it's hard to really feel the support sometimes. I feel on my own, like I am pulling people along.

155

A Story About the Enthusiast/Epicure (7)

Chole (assumed name) was always asked to plan her friends' parties, to be the bride's maid, to join the group at the bar. She had a hard time saying no to any of these requests, she never wanted to lose her place as the girl in the center of the excitement, or worse, to let anyone down.

She was exhausted. It showed on her face. Still, for the first 2 hours of this weekend workshop, she had been multi-tasking and checking her phone. Finally, the workshop leader had to ask for our cell phones to be turned off. She sheepishly complied. She was nervous to have her phone off, you could see her checking it then remembering it was off and shaking her head.

Chole came to this weekend based on her counselor's advice. Her fiancé had ended things. She was really upset, saying she did not understand why he left. She thought it was going well. Later we learned he said he didn't feel like he was a priority and couldn't see them having a family. But that's what she wanted, a family. He said he was just more ready for their dream than she was and he couldn't see her handling it all. He had been asking her to set a date for a while.

With no distractions, from the outside world this young woman started looking like she felt: tired, confused, hurt. Late in the day, it was her turn to speak during an exercise. The leader started by asking her what she was missing in life, and to start to set priorities to understand what mattered to her. To do this with no judgment, simply give herself time to feel what was real for her, not what the world wanted from her.

It was an arduous task for her to sit with her own feelings. But life is not always happy, and excitement is not always meaningful or satisfying.

Chole, got to a point in that group to see that without the depth, the meaning was lost. I hope she is continuing to balance excitement and depth.

Tools for The Enthusiast/Epicure (7)

➤ Take short self-assessment breaks to "check in" during the day.
  o Do I feel like I am pushing through?
  o Am I grounded – not rushing, feet on and ground, bringing my ideas to reality?
  o Am I overbooked, can I push myself less and enjoy what I am doing with more fullness?
➤ Breath – give yourself some space inside.
  o Follow that breath until you feel the pleasure of release of tension in the body.
➤ You are temptable!
  o Know this about yourself and almost always avoid saying yes to other's ideas and plans too quickly.
    ▪ Take a breath, feel the answer in your body.
    ▪ Consider the real cost of invite.
    ▪ And don't let others cajole you to their will.
➤ Have a plan for yourself.
  o Find a way to organize the areas of your life.
  o Look at mind mapping and other creative tools to help you:
    ▪ Prioritize what you want to focus your energy on.
    ▪ Regarding the people in your world. Consider their place in your life and if you want to expand, contract, or maintain that relationship.
    ▪ Is it healthy for you to combine socializing and exercise?
    ▪ Or is it better for you to make that quiet time?
➤ Take time to care for your body and emotions, they are part of you!
  o Don't fear emotional pain. It is part of being human.
➤ Think through the stages or steps of your plan.
  o Consider if you want to carry it through to fruition. This helps you to avoid many partially done projects.
➤ *Thoughtful Actions + Vision = Creation*

157

Enthusiast/Epicure (7) Arrows

Use Traits from Style Perfectionist/Reformer (1)

➢ When a 7 positively accesses the Perfectionist/Reformer energy they take charge of their mind and use the grounded body-based energy of the 1.

➢ This enables them to get things done, be thorough and pay attention to details.

➢ 1s usually have great self-control, this is a boon to the 7.

Use traits from style intellectual/investigator (5)

➢ 5 think deeply about subjects. This quality enables the 7 to thoroughly consider their ideas.

➢ It brings the 7 inwards, helps them to understand the choices they are making.

➢ A mature 7 will slow down and calculate the risks of a venture. They will still adventure, but with mindfulness, mitigating the risks while enjoying the reward.

Enthusiast/Epicure (7) Wings

Enthusiast/Epicure (7) w/ Loyal Skeptic (6) wing

➢ Outgoing, friendly, easy to get along with.
➢ Very productive, cooperative, compassionate towards others.
➢ Big picture, humanitarian.
➢ Feels inferior when loses position in the group.
➢ Likes to entertain.
➢ Can become manic.

Enthusiast/Epicure (7) w/ Challenger/Influencer (8) wing

➢ High energy, unstoppable.
➢ Hard working but can become aggressive.
➢ Practical, grounding of the big picture.
➢ Adventurous but can be reckless.
➢ Seeks intensity but can burn out on the world. This can lead to disappointment, melancholy or destructive behavior.

About The Challenger/Influencer (8)

- 8s want to be influential, to matter.
- They can be confrontive. They are nicknamed the Challenger/Influencer for a reason.
- It is in their nature to push boundaries, to recreate things in their own image: to leave their mark.
- Another nickname is protector. With some 8s you are in or out. They are rarely neutral.
- Fearing them only makes matters worst. If you fear them, they can't trust you.
- 8s are often willing to take on leadership, even in tough situations.
- With massive amounts of physical energy, the 8 is a powerhouse of a person and a strong personality.
- Some are very emotional and soft with those close to them.
- When they let themselves feel vulnerable with people the best of them comes out.
- They want you to meet them with power and conviction.
- "It is by testing the boundaries of a person, that you know their true spirit."
- Why are people so weak?
- I am a nice person, I want to be liked and cared for, but I don't want to be weak or needy!
- You can't trust a person you can control. However, to lead you must be able and willing to control some people.
- There are clear lines between my team/country and yours. You will have to prove you're my ally, and I have to remain alert, suspicious because I must stay in power.
- I wish people weren't afraid of me.
- It is so much fun to be in charge. I enjoy watching over my kingdom, doing things for my people, having authority.
- Let's get this done! It is fun to see my impact on the world.

A Story About the Challenger/Influencer (8)

Growing up before title IX and girl power, being a Challenger woman was tough. Born in 1964 I was taught that girls are about who they marry. I wanted to be President, not be told what to do! I was often told to tone myself down, that ladies don't talk so loudly, that I would not find a man if I didn't let him win. Why would I want a man who would be upset if won, or who wasn't able to stand up and win sometimes? I admit I was caught up in what I was taught because our culture impacts us at a subconscious level. I Challenged the imposed cultural limitations.

Being a Challenger means that there are times when you don't understand people's reactions to you. It is normal for me to just say what I mean, sometimes it comes out stronger than I realize. It is surprising to see their faces go into upset when I don't mean anything upsetting at all.

Being inside the body of a Powerful Person, I feel sort of like the hulk. It's a feeling that I must be careful not to crush people because they seem to be so delicate. There is a feeling/perception that I must fill in the leadership voids or fill in the places that are left unattended, to be the boss, to things get done. I want to lead, and then there are times I really wish someone would just wrap their arms around me and give me a very long comforting hug. Men Challengers seem more acceptable to our society. Everyone loves a big protective guy with a soft heart.

Challenger are considered age advanced. Playfulness is hard for us because the pressure of making sure we matter, and that we don't lose power leaves little time for silliness. Often, we are too much for people. But when we are needed will step up with our broad leadership shoulders.

As an adult today, being a woman Challenger is much easier, and frankly more fun. I don't have to be a "nice girl" but I have developed myself to find the way to be authentic and gentle. If the situation calls for a tough leader, I can do that too. Part of the fun of self-development is being comfortable in almost all situations.

162

Tools for the Challenger/Influencer (8)

➢ If you choose to be compassionate you will be a great leader.
  o It is easy to get into an echo chamber that makes you feel powerful. This is a very dangerous place to be. In an echo chamber you are most vulnerable, because if just one new idea gets in, your whole world can crumb.
  o Anxiety for you feels like anger sometimes. It is the awareness that you are vulnerable, but trying to act like you aren't.
  o No one is bulletproof, you know this. You know how much you want power and what you are willing to do for it, so you know that there are enemies out there to fight for power.
  o Compassion helps you to see what is really a fight for power and what is you fearing that you have to prove you matter.
  o Study the difference between power vs force choose compassionate power and you will transform from a Challenger/Fighter to a true leader with sustainable power.
➢ You are far more vulnerable than you want to admit. Let people in, choose people you know you can trust (not just people who agree with you).
➢ It is important that you have strong people in your life. Find a counselor, a few friends, a family member, one or more people who don't just agree with you.
➢ You need people who are strong enough to tell you the truth, and you need to listen! Honor and trust those who stand up to you.
➢ Stop defending yourself – it disempowers you while it pushes away your true allies. Be objective about all information and sort it without reaction. Knowledge is powerful equal to the force of your being.
➢ You can gain lasting loyalty and genuine respect through active listening, looking for commonality, and making room for others input.
➢ Power comes from inside of you. The empowerment of self-mastery is stronger than the power drunken effects of power over others.
➢ *Vulnerability + Inner Power = Lasting Power*

Challenger/Influencer (8) Wings

Challenger/Influencer (8) w/ Enthusiast/Epicure (7) wing

- ➢ Blunt communicator.
- ➢ Action-oriented, needs to move, express their power physically.
- ➢ Willing leader.
- ➢ Can be a force for whatever they believe in.
- ➢ Does not accept limitation, blows through them, and proves their power.
- ➢ Can become aggressive or blinded by power.

Challenger/Influencer (8) w/Peacemaker/Mediator (9) wing

- ➢ Subdued power.
- ➢ Determined with thoughtfulness of effects of power on others.
- ➢ Reassuring protector.
- ➢ Bear-like quality, strong but can be plodding.
- ➢ In personal life very cuddly, but at work very aggressive.
- ➢ Can become quietly threatening.

Challenger/Influencer (8) Arrows

Use Traits from Style Helper/Giver (2)

➤ Connect with people.
➤ Care about others, putting other people's needs into their decision making.
➤ Overcoming their own fear of vulnerability enables them to find softness and love. Taming their inner drive for power over others.

Use Traits from Style Intellectual/Investigator (5)

➤ The 8 using the 5 qualities starts to think more deeply, do more research. Uplifting themselves to understand, leading to empowerment.
➤ 5 qualities can bring the need for power over to inward power.

About the Peacemaker/Mediator (9)

- Avoiding chaos makes it appear as if the 9 is not leaning in.
- As leaders, they have a very long decision-making process.
- Considering all their options, looking at the long-term impact of the decision.
- When they say they are working on it, they really are. They struggle because they don't understand that they can't hide from their impact on the world. Pretending to be placid becomes a burden.
- When people or events push on me, I withdraw or avoid the issue.
- The world according to me: "we all enjoy life. No fighting and good food for all!"
- I don't like being pressured about things, but I don't want to be rude.
- People react when I assert myself.
- There is so much information in the world. It is interesting and exciting; how do I incorporate it all?
- For example A peacemaker personality style can appear very passive. However, they are deeply insightful, often very skillful, and see complexity around them, they are capable of more than they appear.
- Their hesitancy to act is based on having data from many sources and being able to perceive the pros and cons of most any course of action. In a situation where there is pressure, or where the 9 may feel at risk of upsetting people, they can become overwhelmed.
- Peacemakers try to manage the outside world to keep everyone at ease, even at their own expense. It is as if they disappear for the sake of keeping things copacetic for others. They fear hurting others.
- It is always key to create a safe workplace, with the Peacemaker this means to make mistakes ok so that it is safe to take a risk, safe to set deadlines and move ahead knowing the employee and the team have the resilience to deal with issues as they arise.
- They have access to a wealth of personal power by calming their own fear of disrupting things or causing chaos.

167

A Story About a Peacemaker/Meditator (9)

Juan was a good business person. He was successful, respected for being friendly, fair, and sharp. Being a 1:1 instinct he was very charming when he was pursuing what he wanted.

His wife was constantly badgering him. He just wanted to relax at home. What did she want from him!?!

Peacemaker/Mediators often think that their people pleasing and acting as if they have no needs makes them easy to get along with; however, many people find it frustrating being with people who evaporate. Juan was extremely reactive to anything that seemed like a criticism.

It turned out what she wanted was interaction. When they were dating, he was interacting more, wooing her, and his attention was very satisfying. But now that his wooing was going into the business she felt tossed aside!

Home was where he went inward and pretended the world was evaporating while he had his wine, his dinner and his time without stimulation. So, she was annoying by the simple fact that she was in his quiet place, every request was seen and felt like a demand, not an interaction. Her heart was aching for the man she fell in love with, but he had secured her and shared his money, what more did she need?

He was repressing a great deal of emotion, fighting to get what he needed, and had subconsciously turned his wife into his enemy.

We got him to accept and express his emotions more easily. It was very important to help him to stop people pleasing thinking that it was going to make the world peaceful – it doesn't! She learned to read his signals and to articulate her desire for loving connection.

The most important things we're learning is about each other's needs, humanizing each other, and strategizing about how to build that bridge and make that a happier, more loving marriage.

Tools for the Peacemaker/Mediator (9)

➤ You are naturally a wise and compassionate person.
  - Avoid being overtly humble. It is not genuine.
  - Avoid playing too small or too big like you need no one and nothing. It's just not true and we all see that.
  - Study compassion, you are already empathic/intuitive, this will help you see how to deal with all you feel in the world.
➤ Admit you have needs. The first of which is to not have too much chaos around you. It's ok to say to the family: I need quiet time now, I am going to go for a walk, to my room, etc.
➤ It's ok to close your door at work, to telecommute, to ask for less drama or more organization.
➤ Don't neutralize yourself. We need people in the world who can have the wide humanist point of view that you do.
➤ It is good to have pleasures in the world. Not to be lost in them, but to have things in the world that bring you comfort and joy.
➤ The world is chaotic. Your voice is needed.
➤ It is a top priority that you put your feelings, needs, and desires in the forefront of your thoughts.
➤ As a 9, you have a world view that needs to be heard and seen.
➤ You can bring peace to a difficult situation by asserting yourself.
➤ It can be hard for you to assert yourself "against" strong personalities, but it is what is needed. You can learn from leaning on your Challenger wing to bring your power into focus.
➤ STOP placating anyone out of fear. If you are coddling bad behavior because you fear upsetting people, you are letting them get away with destructive behavior at your expense.
➤ There is nothing to fear in "disruption". It is inevitable. If you are placating, you are already living in fear. People need to hear reason, you can't allow them to persist especially if they are doing harm to people you care about or oversee. Also look at self!
➤ *Wisdom + Action = Success*

Peacemaker/Mediator (9) Wings

Peacemaker/Mediator (9) w/ Challenger/Influencer (8) wing

> - Usually more humble than justified.
> - Avoid harming anyone, aware of their power to do harm they choose the position of the "gentle giant".
> - Avoids own vulnerability.
> - Can become isolated, defensive, lose touch with reality and hide away.

Challenger/Influencer (9) w/Perfectionist/Reformer (1) wing

> - Tends towards dreaming of a perfect world based on higher ideals.
> - Caring but not very emotive.
> - Holds self and others to a high standard.
> - Capable of organizing many schools of thought.
> - Cares about people doing what is best for all.
> - Can become manic about their passions.

Peacemaker/Mediator (9) Arrows

Use Traits from Style Achiever/Performer (3)

- ➤ Lean into projects.
- ➤ Increase your energy and excitement in the world.
- ➤ Engaging in priorities.
- ➤ Embrace leadership and expression.

Use Traits from Style Loyal Skeptic (6)

- ➤ The 9 can choose to develop analytical ability without getting lost in it.
- ➤ The 6 quality of loyalty can help the 9 be decisive and set principals that guide them.

THRIVING VS SURVIVING

Humans thrive when:

> ➤ They are safe, supported and connected.
> ➤ To create these conditions:
> ➤ Teams communicate, inquire, agree.
> ➤ All human beings face fears both real and imagined. These put us in survival mode.

We can empower ourselves with the self-awareness to tell if we are in survival mode based on:

> ➤ Our thoughts.
> ➤ Our emotional State.
> ➤ Our behaviors.
> ➤ Peoples' responses to us.

We have the power to rise above survival mode.

Usually, survival mode is triggered when we feel that our egos, our thoughts, or ideas are threatened. We all forget that these are not us, these are things our minds create, but we are not in life-threatening danger, so survival mode is destructive because fear does not create an uplifting outcome.

Attaching too heavily to our own ideas kills curiosity.

Innovation, personal success, and creative problem solving require an agile mind, just as logistics and planning require a focused mind.

The majority of what puts us in survival mode can be resolved with self-awareness, curiosity about ourselves, and empowered action.

Use the information in the Enneagram to help you determine if you are thriving or surviving.

Use the tools you're being given to shift yourself into thriving.

Ideas for using this information:

Look at the qualities of your home-base type and other significant numbers in your Enneagram.

Assess yourself:

Do I act that way?

Do I think that way?

Am I being upfront with myself? Or am I making myself ok?

Do people say I am that way? Or do they respond to me as if I am that way?

You can be private and honest about this. Some people use a journal to track their self-discoveries.

We all go to the survival side of our styles. You empower yourself when you choose to see these things.

When you decide what to focus on, switching to the thriving side, use one or more the tools you've been given or refer to the tool guide (to be published soon).

By learning about all the styles you can understand what others' behavior's reveal about how they feel.

This is a great time to use curiosity about the other person and about yourself. Curiosity is powerful and keeps us present: Wonder what is happening for them, and if appropriate ask them.

Never put anyone on the spot and respect everyone's varying needs for privacy.

When you see others struggling or in survival mode, try to create a safer space for them.

Often the diplomatic and respectful act of acknowledging an emotional, tone, or body language as sign of discomfort is all that is needed to release the tension. IE: Is there something else you would like to bring to the conversation? Or: What do you need for this conversation to be more comfortable or productive? Etc.

Sometimes simply backing off and giving a person a chance to regain composure is enough to for them to self-correct.

BUT…. don't push if you see someone struggling. This only serves to increase the intensity of survival mode.

It's ok if you or both of you are struggling to take a break.

Productivity time is lost if you are pushing through instead of clearing up an emotional issue.

Following are charts that provide insight about what a person is experiencing and/or demonstrating when they are thriving or surviving.

The thriving areas are on top and the surviving are on the bottom.

When a person is thriving, they feel safe, connected and know their purpose.

When a person is surviving there is something happening in them pushing them into fear.

Graphs of each type in Thriving and Surviving

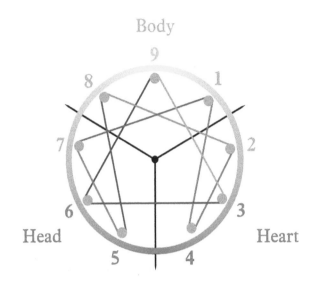

Perfectionist/ Reformer (1)

Helper/Giver (2)

Achiever/Performer (3)

Romantic/Individualist (4)

Intellectual/Investigator (5)

Loyal Skeptic (6)

Enthusiast/Epicure (7)

Challenger/Influencer (8)

Peacemaker/Mediator (9)

On the following pages you will find original graphics designed to help you visually learn more about and integrate the work we have done in this book.

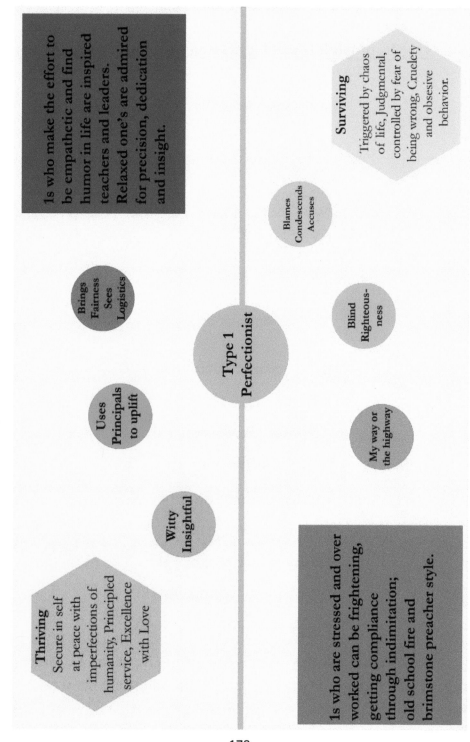

Type 1 Perfectionist

1s who make the effort to be empathetic and find humor in life are inspired teachers and leaders. Relaxed one's are admired for precision, dedication and insight.

Surviving
Triggered by chaos of life, Judgmental, controlled by fear of being wrong, Cruelty and obsesive behavior.

Blames Condescends Accuses

Brings Fairness Sees Logistics

Blind Righteous-ness

Uses Principals to uplift

My way or the highway

Witty Insightful

Thriving
Secure in self at peace with imperfections of humanity, Principled service, Excellence with Love

1s who are stressed and over worked can be frightening, getting compliance through indimitation; old school fire and brimstone preacher style.

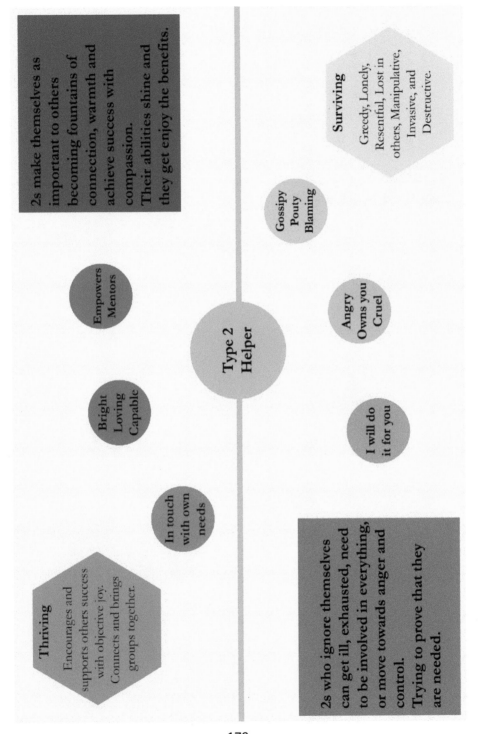

2s make themselves as important to others becoming fountains of connection, warmth and achieve success with compassion. Their abilities shine and they get enjoy the benefits.

Surviving

Greedy, Lonely, Resentful, Lost in others, Manipulative, Invasive, and Destructive.

Gossipy
Pouty
Blaming

Empowers
Mentors

Angry
Owns you
Cruel

Type 2 Helper

Bright
Loving
Capable

I will do it for you

In touch with own needs

Thriving

Encourages and supports others success with objective joy. Connects and brings groups together.

2s who ignore themselves can get ill, exhausted, need to be involved in everything, or move towards anger and control.
Trying to prove that they are needed.

179

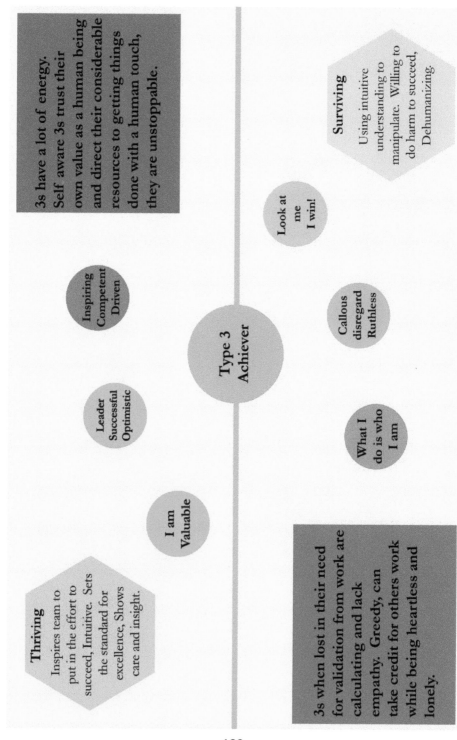

3s have a lot of energy. Self aware 3s trust their own value as a human being and direct their considerable resources to getting things done with a human touch, they are unstoppable.

Surviving
Using intuitive understanding to manipulate. Willing to do harm to succeed, Dehumanizing.

Look at me I win!

Inspiring Competent Driven

Type 3 Achiever

Callous disregard Ruthless

Leader Successful Optimistic

What I do is who I am

I am Valuable

Thriving
Inspires team to put in the effort to succeed, Intuitive. Sets the standard for excellence, Shows care and insight.

3s when lost in their need for validation from work are calculating and lack empathy. Greedy, can take credit for others work while being heartless and lonely.

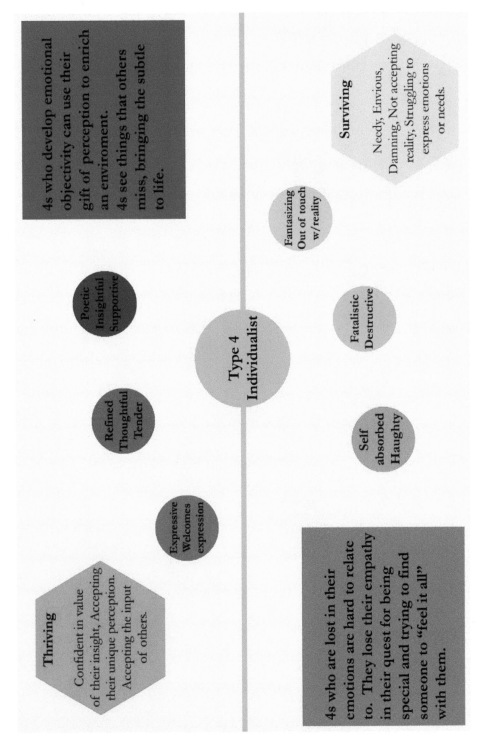

Type 4
Individualist

4s who develop emotional objectivity can use their gift of perception to enrich an enviroment. 4s see things that others miss, bringing the subtle to life.

Surviving

Needy, Envious, Damning, Not accepting reality, Struggling to express emotions or needs.

Fantasizing Out of touch w/reality

Poetic Insightful Supportive

Refined Thoughtful Tender

Fatalistic Destructive

Self absorbed Haughty

Expressive Welcomes expression

Thriving

Confident in value of their insight, Accepting their unique perception. Accepting the input of others.

4s who are lost in their emotions are hard to relate to. They lose their empathy in their quest for being special and trying to find someone to "feel it all" with them.

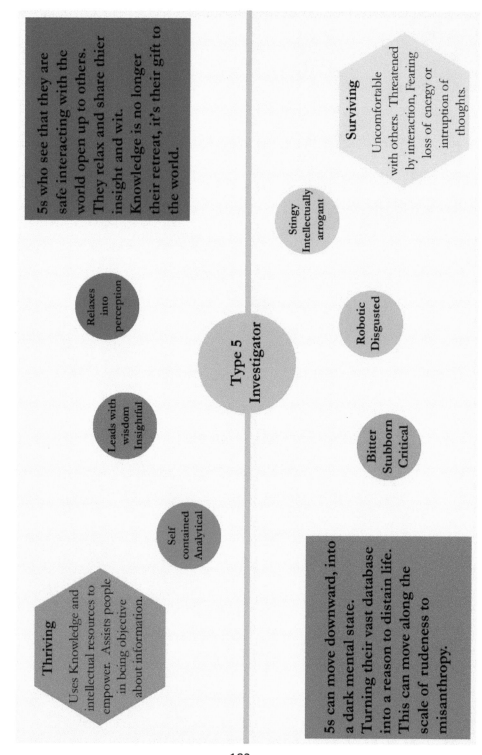

Thriving

Uses Knowledge and intellectual resources to empower. Assists people in being objective about information.

5s who see that they are safe interacting with the world open up to others. They relax and share thier insight and wit. Knowledge is no longer their retreat, it's their gift to the world.

Relaxes into perception

Leads with wisdom Insightful

Self contained Analytical

Type 5 Investigator

Stingy Intellectually arrogant

Robotic Disgusted

Bitter Stubborn Critical

Surviving

Uncomfortable with others. Threatened by interaction, Fearing loss of energy or intruption of thoughts.

5s can move downward, into a dark mental state. Turning their vast database into a reason to distain life. This can move along the scale of rudeness to misanthropy.

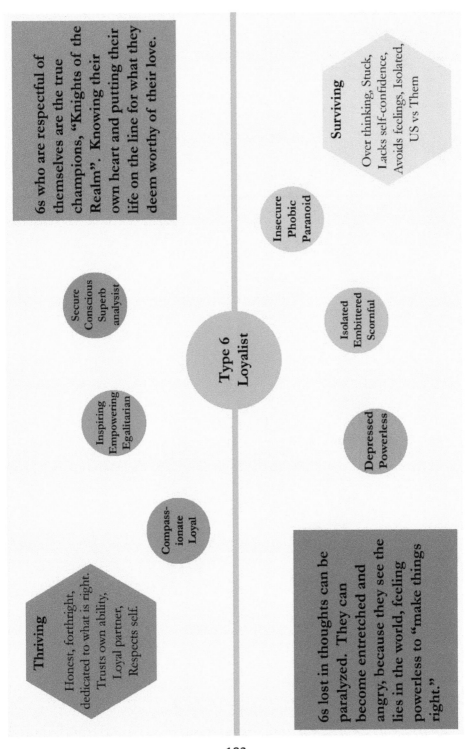

Thriving

Honest, forthright, dedicated to what is right. Trusts own ability, Loyal partner, Respects self.

Compassionate Loyal

Inspiring Empowering Egalitarian

Secure Conscious Superb analysist

Type 6 Loyalist

Insecure Phobic Paranoid

Isolated Embittered Scornful

Depressed Powerless

Surviving

Over thinking, Stuck, Lacks self-confidence, Avoids feelings, Isolated, US vs Them

6s who are respectful of themselves are the true champions, "Knights of the Realm". Knowing their own heart and putting their life on the line for what they deem worthy of their love.

6s lost in thoughts can be paralyzed. They can become entretched and angry, because they see the lies in the world, feeling powerless to "make things right."

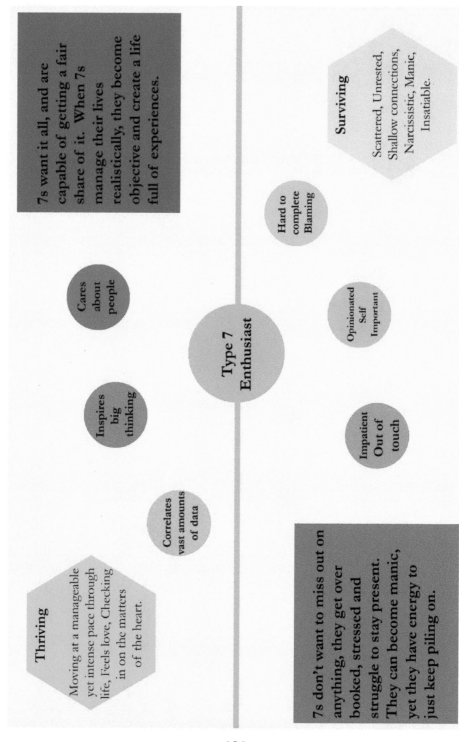

Thriving

Moving at a manageable yet intense pace through life, Feels love, Checking in on the matters of the heart.

Correlates vast amounts of data

Inspires big thinking

Cares about people

Type 7 Enthusiast

7s want it all, and are capable of getting a fair share of it. When 7s manage their lives realistically, they become objective and create a life full of experiences.

Surviving

Scattered, Unrested, Shallow connections, Narcissistic, Manic, Insatiable.

Hard to complete Blaming

Opinionated Self Important

Impatient Out of touch

7s don't want to miss out on anything, they get over booked, stressed and struggle to stay present. They can become manic, yet they have energy to just keep piling on.

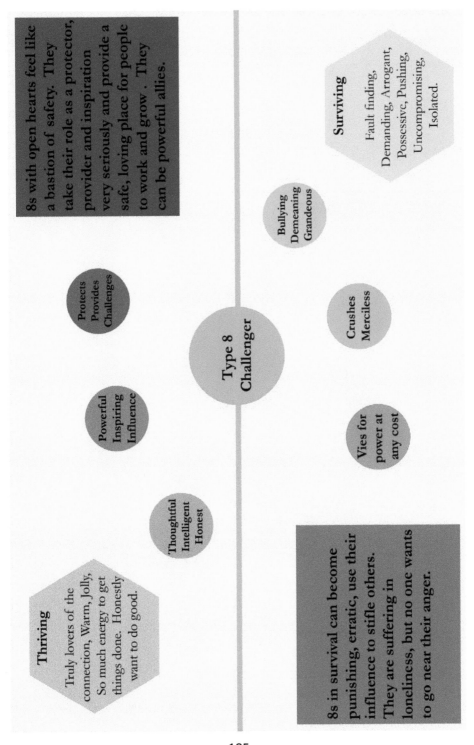

Type 8 Challenger

8s with open hearts feel like a bastion of safety. They take their role as a protector, provider and inspiration very seriously and provide a safe, loving place for people to work and grow. They can be powerful allies.

Surviving

Fault finding, Demanding, Arrogant, Possessive, Pushing, Uncompromising, Isolated.

Bullying Demeaning Grandeous

Protects Provides Challenges

Crushes Merciless

Powerful Inspiring Influence

Vies for power at any cost

Thoughtful Intelligent Honest

Thriving

Truly lovers of the connection, Warm, Jolly, So much energy to get things done. Honestly want to do good.

8s in survival can become punishing, erratic, use their influence to stifle others. They are suffering in loneliness, but no one wants to go near their anger.

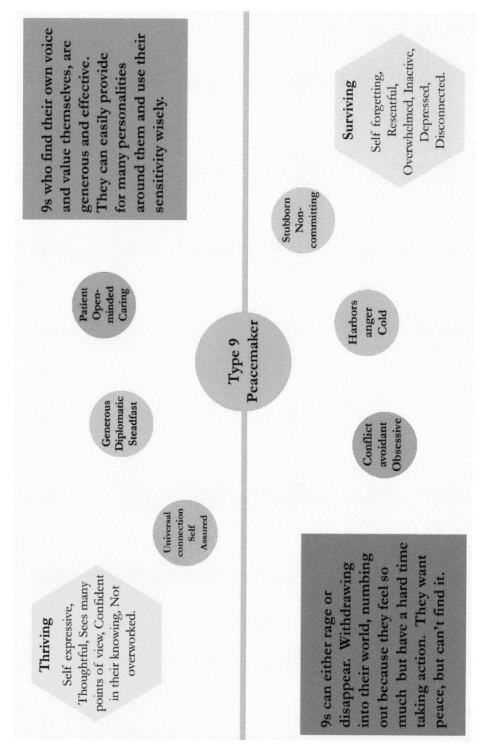

Thriving

Self expressive, Thoughtful, Sees many points of view, Confident in their knowing, Not overworked.

9s who find their own voice and value themselves, are generous and effective. They can easily provide for many personalities around them and use their sensitivity wisely.

Surviving

Self forgetting, Resentful, Overwhelmed, Inactive, Depressed, Disconnected.

Patient
Open-minded
Caring

Stubborn
Non-committing

Type 9 Peacemaker

Harbors anger
Cold

Generous
Diplomatic
Steadfast

Conflict avoidant
Obsessive

Universal connection
Self Assured

9s can either rage or disappear. Withdrawing into their world, numbing out because they feel so much but have a hard time taking action. They want peace, but can't find it.

RECAP

If we learn to have compassion when people are in survival mode, we can create a more productive workplace, and better personal relationships because we all feel safer.

We also can stop taking other people's struggles personally, and become allies in productive behavior:

supporting, encouraging, and using the important messages that our emotions provide; while we learn to be objective about the destructive, fearful, emotional reactions that waste drain our resources.

Don't waste energy pushing through noncreative, combative, or emotional resistance.

➢ Step back.
➢ Access.
➢ Breathe.
➢ Release the tension or internal resistance.
➢ Take personal responsibility.
➢ See that you are safe.
➢ Accept and Forgive/Let Go.
➢ Say what needs to be said about the difficulty.
➢ Move back onto the task.
➢ Practice this and it will become natural.

"Our task must be to free ourselves by widening our circle of compassion to embrace all living creatures and the whole of nature and its beauty."

- Albert Einstein

Authors Bio:

Naomi Eklund

Coach Mentor Trainer Author Speaker

Infinite Yes Coaching, Inc. Founder

www.infiniteyesinc.com

Infinite Yes Productions, Inc. Founder

Inspiring Tools and Media

www.infiniteyesproductions.com

I studied psychology at the University of Illinois, Chicago Campus. Since I was a young woman, I have studied personal growth and development. It is my passion. Learning to understand people, to see what makes the human mind tick and how to improve lights me up.

In 1997 when my son was born, I took my part time coaching work and turned it into my full-time practice. I wanted to be the one to raise my kid, and I needed to work flexible hours. My son was the angel baby who slept on a regular schedule, so much so that I scheduled client calls around his naps!

In 2001 I took my first Enneagram workshop and was hooked. It was a challenging but useful tool and I liked that it didn't make people feel stuck in their style but used the personality style as a way to understand the whole person.

Since then, I have taken many workshops, trainings, read extensivity and started practicing it with clients about 8 years ago. It is a game changer with Clients because it gives them an excellent mirror for themselves and it's like an encyclopedia for others. It's very helpful to understand. When we bother to understand we have knowledge and practicing behaviors ased on good information becomes wisdom. I like wisdom, it makes life asier.

n my practice, I serve people from CEOs of international companies, to ntrepreneurs, to stay at home parents. I love creating trainings and onsulting about ways to improve the team and company culture.

The principals of being human remain the same in the workplace and the ome. If we understand people and principals of interaction, we have etter relationships.

ixing your relationships and doing preventative maintenance is my joy in ife, and it provides more productive and loving lives.

3orn with a strong intuitive and empathic connection, I have always been ble to help people heal, to help them suffer less. My life's work has been o study humans, to experience and teach tools that make healing easier, nore effective and more sustainable. Suffering is part of life, but if we earn from it does not need to continue.

love getting people to the point where they are preemptive about their ives, avoiding suffering before it happens.

am a follower of the Principals of Conscious Capitalism Mindful Business Practices and the Triple Bottom Line. In this, I have founded Infinite Yes Productions, Inc. Our goal is to inspire, to keep our products affordable, pay our artists and staff well, and have fun uplifting people.

My life is blessed in so many ways. I have turned the challenges of life into chances to learn, and helped many grow into happier lives. It is rewarding to see a couple gain the light of understanding and to watch a team take the information you give them to work together better. One of my favorite tasks is to take a young manager and help them gain the emotional intelligence to become a great leader.

Thank you for reading this book. I would love to connect with you. If you have questions or comments, please reach out to me.

Infinite Yes Productions and Infinite Yes Coaching, Inc. is committed to the arts and artist worldwide.

Too often people think that they are not artistic. I feel sad about how often I hear people say, "I am not creative". Perhaps this is why we forget the arts because we don't see their relativeness in our lives, or we don't know how to relate to the arts to meet our survival needs. But the arts help to lift us beyond the notion that everything is scarce, they show us the part of us that lives unapologetically for the sake of expressing. The arts take courage, they are a risk.

I don't believe we can advance without the mental-emotional challenge of the arts and feel sure we can't advance spiritually without the courage to create things anew in the world. Art is to give a bit of the Divine through our own being, to share and contribute. Your art might be a gorgeous spreadsheet, a sturdy building, or perfectly cozy home.

This book is alive in part due to the artistry of Patrick Coan of Spectri and Jachob Wolff of Jachob Wolff Imagery. Patrick joined my team 5 years ago when I was starting to implement my renewed vision after a few life changing events. He is the visual genius behind my website(s) and without his getting my vision, I don't know if I could have come this far. He created the logo's with just a few instructions from a dream I shared. Jachob is my son, a gifted photographer and graphic designer. He made the book look amazing and contributed heavily to the design.

Jennifer, my amazing friend, stepped up and said YES, I think this is where I want to be. Giving me much needed and appreciated the support. She is an artist of love and life and making practical things happen with the grace of fairy dust. We still don't know her exact title, because she has so much to offer, what we do know is that she is amazing and gave me and Infinite Yes much-needed friendship, love, and "got the vision".

Give to the arts

Giving to the community is part of being a good business citizen.

There is no end of abundance or of need. Bringing our abundance to heal the need brings more players into the game.

Infinite Yes Productions, Inc. Is committed to giving a percentage of our profits to the arts.

Tiger Lion Arts (read more below) will be a beneficiary of a portion of the sale of this book. The exact percentage of the gift will be determined by the volume of sales and our profit from sales of the book. This is our first time out.

My goal as a startup company and author is approximately 5% of profit to the arts. To pay my staff and artist above market, making sure that they receive equitable benefits from the fruit of their labor.

If all companies gave to the arts, to those in need, to projects that enriched their community, our lives would all be greatly improved. Below is information on Tiger Lion Arts. As our promoted arts beneficiary, I encourage you to learn more about their work and bring their interactive plays to your communities.

 TigerLion Arts

TigerLion Arts is a Minneapolis-based theater company. We celebrate the wisdom of humans and the spirit of nature through artistic works that awaken, inform and delight communities. We serve people of all ages, origins, perspectives, and abilities, and inspire them to take positive action in their lives and in the world.

For more information go tigerlion.org, join us on Facebook, or email to info@tigerlion.org.

So, trust your art, trust your creative force,

it is your soul manifesting through your doing.

Testimonials

"It is rare that you come across an amazing talent like Naomi-Marie, she is insightful and supportive. I have had the pleasure of working with her for many years and we have collaborated on several projects. I am always impressed by her ability to help others through her innate understanding of human nature, and especially using the Enneagram. Her new book, "Building Bridges Between Personalities, Introducing the Enneagram" is a helpful reference to build more effective relationships, both in the workplace and at home.
I highly recommend her work."

Rosie Potestio
Certified Inter-Faith Spiritual Director

"Naomi's ability to distill information in a manner that is understood and profoundly comprehended by the individual is one of her many strengths. As a coach she is able to be clear, direct and effective.
Learning discipline and developing skills that made me a better professional, partner, mother, and person were all gifts I received from working with Naomi."

Velveth Schmitz
City Council Member at City of Rolling Hills Estates

"Naomi is a mastermind of intuition and empathic understanding. She has the uncanny ability to see beneath the surface and promote solutions towards complex human ailments. She practices relentless enthusiasm for human connection, especially as it relates to an individual's or a group's efficacy and daily interactions. In my professional interaction with Naomi, I have witnessed her knack to see the big picture and desire to tackle the details, as well as her ability to create solutions between disparate domains.

I wholeheartedly recommend Naomi for anyone seeking growth and understanding in themselves and interactions with others."

Patrick Coan
Animation and Technical Director at Bent Image Labs

"I have read a few books on the Enneagram, and multiple self-improvement and inspirational books so I feel I can recommend a good read. This is the bullet point book on what it is all about. Super easy to understand and quick read. I was able to absorb the profound information effortlessly and use it right away in my work situations....and personal situations, too! It would a great to use for office and team building. Can't wait for the workbook! "

Krista Walker
Principal Broker at Coldwell Banker Pro West Real Estate

"Naomi is passionate about her mission to bring positivity to the world through teaching about compassion. It is inspiring to see her vision helping so many. She is uplifting and encouraging while she informs and challenges. It is powerful and life-changing. "

Jennifer Kuns
Administrative Assistant

"As a self-employed business owner I have garnered priceless key insights and a deeper awareness of what motivates us as a society from "You Using the Enneagram." All of these have been invaluable to further my success with my clients as well as my interpersonal relationships."

JC

Entertainment Industry
Consultant

"I've known Naomi for over ten years and I can say she is a person that is very passionate about anything she does. We did some life coaching work together, and her incite was ineradicable. She has a warm caring style, but still brings the point across. Her insight lets clients learn things about themselves and build skills that they didn't know they had. Empowering people to become the best version of themselves, just great.

I highly recommend Naomi for team building, but also for personal coaching."

Florian Geiger-Taussig
Business Development at Bioelektra Group

"Naomi has provided invaluable leadership coaching and team training services for many members of our management team.

The Enneagram (personality style assessment) provides a really useful construct to help leaders understand other managers' and their own employees' perspectives.

Naomi's coaching has helped us reduce conflict between and among teams so we can get more done with less drama!"

Carol Adams
Vice President Health Operations, Fringe Benefits Group, Austin, Texas

RESOURCES

Please visit my website:

www.infiniteyesinc.com

www.infiniteyesrpoductions.com

To read blogs, learn about classes, arrange a personal consultation or contact us to work with your company.

My Focus is Building Bridges Between People and people relate through personality; the logical progression is the more we understand our own and others' personalities, the easier it is to develop intelligence about each other and make choices that increase purpose, connection, and happiness. Releasing our souls to lead in our lives.

Contact us at naomi@infiniteyesinc.com to arrange for an assessment, report, and review session.

Arrange a consultant to go over and explain the results and/or

My YouTube Channel: Naomi Eklund

Find me on LinkedIn and Facebook.